Mortgage Free
Debt Free

Mortgage Free, Debt Free

5 Steps To The Fast Track

Industry secrets you must know.

Michael Lee

Published by
Franky Pinklestone
P.O. Box 134,
MORISSET New South Wales 2264
www.frankypinklestone.com

Edited by Sasha Tohme
Cover art by Lyndal Frollano

National Library of Australia Cataloguing-in-Publication entry:

Author:	Lee, Michael, 1967.
Title:	Mortgage Free, Debt Free: 5 Steps To The Fast Track: Industry secrets you must know / by Michael Lee.
ISBN:	978-0-646-55033-6
Subjects:	Lee, Michael, 1967 Finance, Personal Debt House buying--Finance.

National Library of Australia.

Dewey Decimal Classification notation: 332.02402

The aim of this book is to provide general information about money, debt and mortgages. While every effort has been made to ensure that the contents are accurate and current, the information only reflects that which was available at the time of writing. Information in this book is in no way intended to replace or supersede professional advice. Neither the author nor the publisher may be held responsible for any action or claim resulting from the use of this book or information contained in it.

All savings and costs calculations are based on a 30 year principal and interest loan of $379,000 and interest rate of 7.15% p.a. assuming minimum monthly payments unless otherwise stated.

Printed in the USA

Dedicated to my family and friends who love and support me.

CONTENTS

Forward by Scott Pape, the Barefoot Investor

Years ago, on a cold Sunday afternoon, I was sitting at my PC searching Google: "independent mortgage broker", "fee-for-service mortgage broker", "mortgage broker who won't rip me off". Eventually, after kissing many cyber-frogs, I found Michael Lee's site.

It described him as a 'mortgage researcher' – whatever the hell that meant. Still, I was curious enough to email him, and then forgot all about him, as you tend to do on the internet.

Everything changed the next morning when I received a call from Michael. We spoke for over an hour about the tricks and traps that confront borrowers, and generally bagged out an industry that is slanted towards salespeople. His passion for the subject was infectious (and to this day I haven't met anyone who can talk for hours on interest rate differential pricing like Michael).

What really shocked me about Michael, though, was his integrity. People like him are few and far between in the money game. In an industry that gets paid more the more money you borrow, Michael follows the two golden Barefoot principles of borrowing: the amount a bank will lend you is usually more than you should borrow, and owning your home outright – getting the banker off your back – is something everyone should aspire to.

Not only has Michael's advice saved me tens of thousands of dollars over the years, he's done the same for my family and friends. Whenever anyone I care about needs to deal with a bank, I refer them to Michael.

Why?

Because I know they're in good hands. He has the ability to cut through the misleading jargon and get to the bare bones of what really matters in a mortgage: low costs, flexibility, and above all else safety.

Michael is an independently wealthy bloke whose passion in life is cleaning up the home loan market.

It's a worthy goal. After all, buying a home is the biggest financial decision most people will ever make – and that's why you need this book. It'll potentially save you tens of thousands of dollars. Even better, it will open your eyes to how the real game of money is played.

Scott Pape, the Barefoot Investor

"Make all you can,
save all you can,
give all you can."

John Wesley
1703 – 1791

Introduction

I have been told by at least one highly successful author that to sell books I should write more about me and insert it here. However Mortgage Free, Debt Free is about you and quite frankly, writing about myself makes me feel like a bit of a boorish plonker. So if my book tanks, I'll know that they were right and I was wrong, which for me still beats feeling like a plonker hands down.

Even though I have spoken, written and been published quite a bit over the years, selling books is not my area of expertise.

My specialty is educating people about credit - the real story. Unearthing the ins and outs, the tricks, the traps and the profit boosting secrets of the mortgage industry that quietly eat away at your wealth.

This book teaches you how to use this knowledge to become mortgage free and debt free as fast as possible while still enjoying life.

If you want to learn more about me and my decade or so spent working in and upsetting the finance industry, flip to the last page of this book. However from my perspective, you and getting your mortgage right really should come first, so let's get on with it.

I promise that regardless of your current financial knowledge, by the time you finish Mortgage Free, Debt Free you will be able to:

- ✓ Slash the time and money wasted on your mortgage.
- ✓ Choose only the right loan features for your next loan.
- ✓ Easily compare any loan with any other loan.
- ✓ Reduce and avoid mortgage stress.
- ✓ Eliminate debt faster. Reach financial freedom sooner.

If you are like most borrowers, your mortgage is the largest financial commitment of your life. Purchase a property using a 50% deposit and you could spend more money in interest than you did on the property itself. Borrow 80% and the numbers get even bigger.

Small mistakes can cost thousands. Make a few and they really start to add up. You pay for each mistake with money which may not be the centre of your universe, however, you earn that money through sacrificing time spent living for time spent working. While you can usually earn more money, you can never get more time. And time, dear reader, is what we use to measure life. Your life.

> *"Time = Life, Therefore, waste your time and waste your life"*
> *Alan Lakein*

The good news is that this book helps you slash the time and money it takes to repay your mortgage. Just how much you will save is up to you as it's your mortgage, your life and your race to run. However soon enough you will have the right tools and knowledge to run faster and more easily than ever before.

Why Mortgage Free, Debt Free is different.

Well for starters, I wrote it so other than examples of bank and broker behaviour, it's a 'spin' free zone. It's not called "how to pay your mortgage off in 7 years" as today's average Australian wouldn't be able to. You'd be hard pressed to do it even if you ate beans for every meal and only ever played slaps for entertainment.

Mortgage Free, Debt Free only contains facts, realistic objectives and innovative ideas that are crucial to your success. Of course owning your property outright in 7 years is a great goal and if that's possible for you, this book gives you a better chance of getting there than any other system. It is easy to understand, simple to do and it works. And as you turn the pages you will begin to understand why it works as well.

Although this book is far from a solo effort, I have worked in and on the mortgage industry since late 2000. I know what can be done.

THE AUSTRALIAN Wednesday September 8 2004

WEALTH

TRUE CONFESSIONS

Picture: James Croucher

Bricks and mortar an early lesson in building capital

Lake Macquarie-based mortgage broker Michael Lee's first investment experience was buying a home

What happened?
It was in 1987 and was actually my first home rather than an investment property — a unit in Dee Why, Sydney. Anyway, interest rates hit an all-time high, the fabled stock market correction took place and I learnt my first significant lesson. I took a loss on total investment of around $18,000 in less than 12 months. The property value slid when interest rates got to the high teens **and I could not afford it. If I had known then what I know now ...**

What are your investment goals?
To continue growing a balanced portfolio with a reasonable level of liquidity allowing me to make adjustments when situations change. And they do.

What's the best investment decision you ever made?
Establishing bSmart three months ago where I am a venture. It was that Dee Why unit. If I still owned it today, even with excellent growth in the Sydney market, the yield would be unacceptably low and the capital gain would have been ordinary. But it taught me several valuable lessons that have paid for themselves a thousand fold. At the moment my key investment is the business, in which my brother and I have invested several hundred thousand dollars plus. Currently this is ahead of schedule. I also own three investment properties in Sydney.

What's the best piece of investment advice you have ever received and who was it from?
A close friend once told me "investment opinions are like armpits, everybody's got them and mostly they stink". Set your own rules, evaluate your performance, always test your thinking, but only with people with proven abilities.

Back in 2004, I was featured in the Wealth section of The Australian to share my investment insights. Although we talked about a few things, I forgot to mention that I am always on the lookout for ways to stretch a dollar, avoid being ripped off and generally get more for less. And that's how Mortgage Free, Debt Free came about.

I have also been a borrower and from time to time I still am, only nowadays I prefer to clear one debt before starting another. You might be a bit more aggressive and hey that's fine, this isn't a property investment book. There are plenty of them already.

Mortgage Free, Debt Free is strictly about managing, limiting, and defeating your largest financial risk and expense regardless of whether you are an investor or an owner-occupier. Your mortgage.

The first time I got one was when I bought an apartment in the late eighties. It was in the beachside suburb of Dee Why on Sydney's Northern Beaches. At almost 20% p.a. mortgage interest rates were outrageous compared to today's, but property prices were a lot lower too.

As impressive as it might be to tell you that I paid that loan off in 3 years, I didn't. Instead I lived. From time to time, I continued to borrow to buy property. I made many mistakes, some of which were not only stupid but expensive too and some of these are captured here.

Fast forward a snitch over a decade to 2001 and I was in the last year of debt for that part of my plan. By 2002, I was debt free, with some property, some passive income, my own slice of paradise and a new plan unfolding.

Although the concept of full time, life long retirement was still just that, a concept, the freedom of owning property with no debt is extraordinary.

Everyone should try it at least once in their lives and preferably as soon as possible which is why I chose to explore the mortgage industry. I didn't have to look too deeply or for too long before I discovered that it promised a heck of a lot more than it delivered and it really needed a shake up.

It still does. The tricks, traps and careless, if not reckless lending are all on the increase.

Doubtless some will find this book confronting, especially if the tricks they use are exposed here. These tricksters will be easy to spot. They will complain they have more experience than I do, moan that I don't know what I am talking about, and may still point out that I have owned brokerage businesses in the past even though I haven't for some years now, and so on.

It's par for the course that tricksters often focus on irrelevant and even false information because they can't honestly argue that bad behaviour does not exist in the mortgage industry. They can't show that increasing regulation does anything but make things worse by lulling some borrowers into a false sense of security.

Besides lots of talking, chest beating and promises, little has changed that genuinely helps you. Neither the industry, regulators nor government have ever provided any real tools that protect you or help you make smarter choices.

The evidence shows that the mortgage industry can and often does squeeze as much money from you as possible. Mortgage Free, Debt Free means they earn less because you end up spending less, which is why this book is one of the few places you will find practical ideas that can make a real, positive difference to your bottom line. To do that, you have to hurt theirs.

As you thumb through the pages, you may see brands that you recognise and some that you may not. I have included them here to demonstrate important points that you need to know and to help you understand the challenges that you face are real even though they may seem quite unbelievable.

In some cases I may have included only one example, however that doesn't mean there aren't many more. There usually are. It's just that I wanted to keep this book short enough for you to learn what you need to without taking a year or two to read it. And just because a lender or a broker appears here, doesn't mean that you should cross them off your list either.

Treat them all equally, without fear or favour, taking each step you are about to learn and using each tool you are about to discover and you will get a better outcome no matter which person or business you deal with.

Apply what you learn and in no time at all, you will be on the path to becoming mortgage free and debt free, which is a wonderful destination.

I look forward to seeing you there.

Part I: Clearing the air

"The most useful piece of learning for the uses of life is to unlearn what is untrue."
Antisthenes (c. 445-c. 365 BCE)

No matter what you think you know you probably need to reset some of your ideas about mortgages, the nuts and bolts and preconceived notions that you may currently have.

This important part is about doing just that.

Oh, just before you turn the page, I should clarify that I use the terms "loan" and "mortgage" interchangeably. The puritans may point out that a mortgage is not a loan, but an instrument. I know that, it's just that most borrowers call their loan a mortgage. So I do too.

The lawless land of mortgages

In 2003, regulator ASIC took a close look at the activities of Mortgage Choice, forming the view that the broker made claims that were misleading and deceptive. These included:

- Mortgage Choice is 'totally unbiased';
- Mortgage Choice provides 'unbiased home loan advice';
- Mortgage Choice consultants are 'paid the same regardless of which lender or loan you choose'.

In May 2004, Mortgage Choice avoided lengthy prosecution by agreeing with ASIC. That same month they won the Australian Banking and Finance "Best Mortgage Broker Award".

Less than a year later, the MIAA awarded Mortgage Choice Retail Aggregator/Originator of the Year. Since then:

- Mortgage Choice continued to promote that it offered "Unbiased advice".
- Mortgage Choice cleverly promoted that it was 'totally impartial' in the years that followed.
- ASIC never did anything about it.
- The industry, including magazines and the MFAA continued to hand out awards to Mortgage Choice.

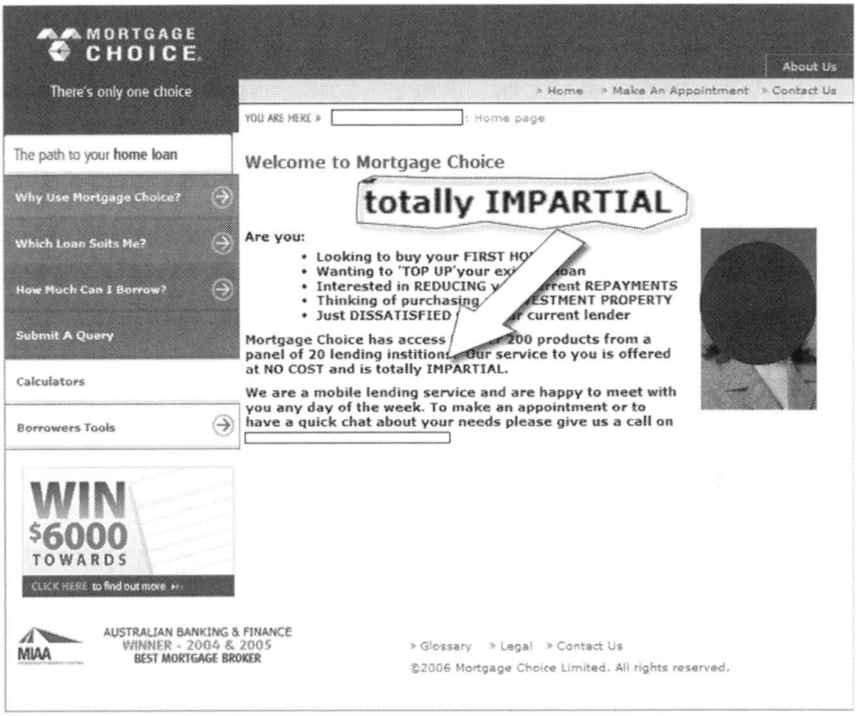

Above: The Mortgage Choice website on 1st September 2006 - two and a half years after the action by ASIC. Below: Mortgage Choice business card collected on 1st September 2006.

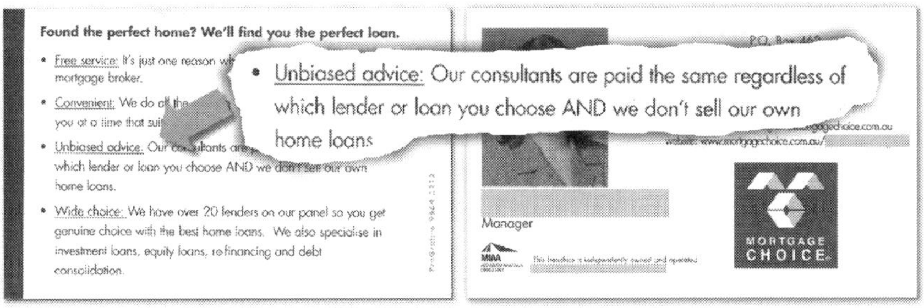

"This information refers only to loans provided by the 27 lenders with whom it has arrangements under which it receives commissions and other payments."

Above: The statement Mortgage Choice agreed to accompany any 'unbiased' reference. It probably should have appeared on the Mortgage Choice website and business cards - even though they switched from 'unbiased' to 'impartial' on their website. It didn't.

An inconvenient truth

With respect to Al Gore, it is an inconvenient truth that lenders and mortgage brokers operate sales businesses. Like the real estate industry they support, they are, at one level or another driven by percentages to make a profit from borrowers. YOU.

It doesn't matter whether the business is a bank, non-bank lender, mortgage originator, or mortgage broker. They all make money if they sell you debt, which is why you should think of them as debt merchants. Granted it's a lot less sexy than the terms they prefer (think mortgage adviser, customer care officer, branch manager etc) but there is no escaping that these people and the businesses they work for make money selling debt. The bigger your debt, the more profit they make. The longer they keep you in debt, the more profit they make.

"Strong communication and selling skills... Uncapped Bonus Scheme"
Hunter United Credit Union seeking a Branch Manager.

While your friendly, professional debt merchant helps you 'achieve your dream', they also have their eyes firmly on your hip pocket to make sure they achieve their dream first. They are backed by teams of well-paid, clever solicitors, sales coaches and marketeers working together to convince you that your merchant's main interest is to help you, but it's not. Staying in business and making a profit both come first. Whenever "looking after you", "staying in business" and "making a profit" clash it's called a conflict of interest and it is a very big problem. In fact, it could be the largest challenge you face when it comes to getting your loan right. A conflict of interest arises whenever a person serves more than one master or mistress and helping one, risks harm to the other.

For example, a mortgage broker remaining true to the promise to protect your interest by choosing the right loan for your needs drastically reduces or destroys that broker's opportunity to make commission. This conflicts with their own interest of paying their bills and making a profit. As we all know, lenders are also very interested in making a profit. So much so, they vary commission and access to their products based on the loyalty and reliability of your broker as a supplier. This means your broker must serve the interest of the lender or risk being cut off and this sets up a serious conflict of interest. Brokers need to look after themselves and make a growing profit. To grow that profit, brokers need to make more money for the lender by selling more to you. To sell to you, brokers simply have to make you think they are giving you the best advice. But will they and who pays the price when they don't?

> *"you will possess outstanding customer service and sales experience... a track record in achieving both individual & team sales targets"*
> *ANZ recruiting for a Personal Banker.*

As for lenders, where they were once tight as a fish's bum when it came to lending money, they now throw it hand over fist at almost anyone wanting to buy residential real estate. They've joined the sales brigade as even banks have franchised out branches in a bid to sell harder, faster. The smiling helper at the branch is often motivated by sales incentives and a counter punch of minimum targets to keep their job. The main difference between lenders and mortgage brokers is that lenders only sell one product range. THEIRS.

You can split hairs on legal mumbo jumbo, however ultimately all these people work for the lender, because that is who pays them or pays the people who pay them. Never forget, broker or lender, their job is to sell. While they've been secreted away in the back rooms transforming to merchants in clever sales mode, borrowers have sat in the dark like mushrooms. Most still thinking of themselves as hopeful borrowers. However, with all that selling going on, the merchants have become very competitive, some in all the wrong ways. It's time to reset what your role is and learn how to make the most of it.

> *"Unfortunately, competition is certainly strong enough, but it is competition on how best to mislead consumers."*
> *John Symond – Aussie Home Loans*

Welcome to the world as seen through the eyes of the merchants; you are now a consumer. A buyer more than borrower. A shopper surrounded by a sea of clever sales merchants. Mortgage Free, Debt Free breaks with tradition. It teaches you how to be smart so you don't ask the salesperson what to buy and how much to spend. After all, why help them meet their sales targets when you are the one footing the bill?

GIGO – An important universal constant

GIGO (pronounced guy-go) is an old computer programmer's term invented so long ago that acronyms had four letters. Nowadays of course, they usually only come with three. GIGO stands for Garbage In, Garbage Out.

> *Wikipedia explains GIGO as "computers will unquestioningly process the most nonsensical of input data and produce nonsensical output. It was most popular in the early days of computing, but applies even more today, when powerful computers can spew out mountains of erroneous information in a short time."*

So what on earth does GIGO have to do with you and your mortgage? It's simple. Computers run on math. The true impact your mortgage has on your life, is also based in math even though the results are far more personal and the symptoms far more emotional.

Every number and every rate out there claiming to simplify your decision, all rely on math. This includes Advertised Comparison Rates, True Rates, Effective Rates, AAPR's, Overall Cost, and any others you encounter.

The questions are:

1. What method has been used?

2. Are all the variables relevant to you included?

3. How accurate and consistent are the formulas?

It's quite fair to say that most formulas reflect the actual way lenders will charge you various fees and costs. However where GIGO becomes important is in the quality of the 'variables' entered into each formula which produces each result. Garbage In, Garbage Out.

In the same way that making small, regular, extra payments slashes the time and money it takes to pay off your loan, changing the loan amount just slightly, excluding a fee or two or tweaking the term can snowball into a massive difference in how much it costs you. What looks cheap might be quite expensive and vice versa.

So the next time you are looking at a nice simple number or rating designed to help you make a decision remember GIGO.

WYSIWYG (pronounced wiz-ee-wig)

An even longer acronym from the ancient annals of computing. It stands for What You See Is What You Get.

It has absolutely nothing to do with the world of mortgages.

Shhh… CLEVER Wordsmiths at work

Woops, sorry, some jargon slipped in there. A wordsmith is, according to the dictionary, a skilled user, or maker of words. So someone like me, but with skill. The problem for you is that you rely on those words to make your decisions. Even if you are not consciously aware, these words influence your belief system.

> *"It is the greatest art of the devil to convince us he does not exist."*
> *Charles Baudelaire French poet (1821 - 1867)*

Clever wordsmiths in marketing departments of merchants and their mates are carefully constructing words with plenty of what I call 'wriggle room'. This is the art of creating a desired impression and still leaving space to say, "Oh, we didn't mean it like that" in case they are caught with their hand in the cookie jar. Of course, that is one BIG 'if' because no one seems to be watching the cookie jar anyway.

Let's take a quick look at a media release from the MIAA, which was picked up and promoted by media across the country. Although the MIAA changed its name to the MFAA, it stayed the same in virtually every other way. So let's stick with their current name, the MFAA. It's an association designed to protect the mortgage industry. The merchants.

> *"To be recognised as Australia"s (sic) pre-eminent association for mortgage and finance professionals"*
> *MFAA's Mission Statement.*

The media release, entitled "MORTGAGE BROKERS PUT CUSTOMERS' INTERESTS FIRST" claimed "Mortgage brokers recommended home loans that are in the best interests of home buyer, (sic) rather than channelling borrowers toward the lending institution that offers the highest commission".

MIAA
MORTGAGE INDUSTRY ASSOCIATION OF AUSTRALIA

MEDIA RELEASE
21.10.2005

PO Box 604
Neutral Bay NSW 2089
T: 1300 554 817
F: 02 9967 2896
www.miaa.com.au

MORTGAGE BROKERS PUT CUSTOMERS' INTERESTS FIRST

Mortgage brokers recommended home loans that are in the best interests of home buyer, rather than channelling borrowers toward the lending institution that offers the highest commission, the Mortgage Industry Association of Australia said today.

Chief Executive of the MIAA, Phil Naylor, said, appropriateness of the product, overall cost benefits, the quality of service and the reputation of the funding organisation were more important factors when a broker made recommendations to customers.

Mr Naylor was refuting an allegation in a recent report that commissions are the single most important factor that brokers consider when deciding which loans to recommend.

"The size of payments made by leading lending institutions to brokers who arrange loans for their customers does not vary greatly. There is no more than 10 basis points difference between the highest and lowest commission that the main lending institutions pay. This represents only $200 or so on the average home loan, which will not prompt the broker to favour one institution because of size of commission," Mr Naylor said.

"It is also instructive that one of the major lending institutions that pays one of the lowest up-front commissions and no trailing commission now accounts for 10 per cent of all new loans issued. Two banks that reduced their commissions last year are now gaining a similar share of new loans that they had before the commission realignments. This would not be the case if brokers simply recommended the loans that paid highest commission," he added.

"The MIAA demands that brokers act in the best interests of their customers. We demand they disclose the commissions they are paid, and this is also law in three of Australia's States. Our members must also disclose any 'soft dollar' or non-commission payments they receive from lending institutions.

"It is common sense that any broker who disregards the interests of their customers and is driven by the highest commission will not have happy customers. As brokers rely on referrals for much of their business, they would not last long in today's competitive environment if they put commission first.

"In fact, we have much research that indicates the use of brokers is rising because of the service they provide."

The Mortgage Industry Association of Australia (MIAA) is the peak body providing service and representation to over 10,000 mortgage brokers, mortgage managers, mortgage lenders (bank and non-bank), and originators to assist them to develop, foster, and promote the mortgage industry in Australia.

The MIAA is dedicated to promoting and maintaining high standards of professionalism and ethical behaviour, and provides a united voice for the industry when required. MIAA strongly emphasises the responsibility that members

The Media Release circulated by the MFAA (then MIAA) explaining their version of commission pressure. Although it makes a point of mentioning trail commissions, it then goes on to ignore the impact.

As evidence, CEO Phil Naylor stated, "The size of payments made by leading lending institutions to brokers who arrange loans for their customers does not vary greatly. There is no more than 10 basis points difference between the highest and lowest commission that the main lending institutions pay. This represents only $200 or so on the average home loan…"

Eliminating the jargon and the wriggle room from this paragraph helps us understand what it really means:

1. "10 basis points" is 0.10%.

2. The average new mortgage back then was $282,000 and corresponds with the "$200 or so on the average home loan…" quoted by the MFAA. Based on the Media Release, vague as it is, the math looks like this:

   $$\$282{,}000 \times 0.10\% = \$282$$

3. Although it is difficult to say which lenders the MFAA nominates as "leading lending institutions", it is hard to argue that any of the big four, which have always had a firm stranglehold on the Australian mortgage market, would ever be excluded by a reasonable person. On that basis, "leading lending institutions" should include:

   - Commonwealth Bank
   - ANZ
   - Westpac
   - National Australia Bank

The very next paragraph of the media release continues:

"It is also instructive that one of the major lending institutions that pays one of the lowest up-front commissions and no trail commission now accounts for 10 per cent of all new loans issued... This would not be the case if brokers simply recommended the loans that paid highest commission".

So let's now eliminate the wriggle room in that lovely slice of gobbledygook. I thought National Australia Bank (NAB) would have to be "one of the major lending institutions that pays one of the lowest upfront commissions and no trail commission". When I asked the MFAA if that lender was NAB, they confirmed that it was.

Now that we have facts to work with, let's set the record straight by reinjecting some important truths:

- Trail commission is paid to brokers on a monthly basis for the life of the loan.

- At the time of the MFAA Media Release, at least one of the big four paid trail commissions of 0.25% p.a. As you now know, National Australia Bank paid and still pays no trail commission.

- You don't have to be Einstein to know that 0.25% minus 0% is not the 0.10% claimed by the MFAA.

- In the example suggested in the MFAA media release, the total commission National Australia Bank would have paid a broker was the upfront rate of 0.5% so:

  $282,000 x 0.5% = $1,410

  That's a once off payment of $1,410. End of sentence, end of story. No trail commission. None, nada, zip.

- However trail commission paid on top of the upfront commission for the "average loan" by the more generous of the big four, <u>in the first five years</u> looks something like this:

  $282,000 x 0.25% x 5 = $3,525

  Of course, trail commission goes on into year six, seven and so on throughout the life of the loan. There is no need to arrange a séance to consult with Einstein. A commission difference of around $3,500 in just the first few years which keeps on growing is not what most people would call "only $200 or so".

No matter which way you slice it, trail payments exceed the commission paid as "upfront" in just a few years. The difference in trail payments offered by lenders including the activation of different features within individual loans can alter trail commissions dramatically over time.

> *"It is common sense that any broker who disregards the interests of their customers and is driven by the highest commission will not have happy customers. As brokers rely on referrals for much of their business, they would not last long in today's competitive environment if they put commission first."*
> *Phil Naylor, Chief Executive Officer, MFAA*

Since the media release, some lenders have reduced commission rates while some lenders have increased them, which means commission pressure has really ramped up.

At the same time, the average new loan has grown by around 34% from $282,000 at the time of the media release to $379,000 in November 2010. This means that, even with 'reduced commissions' merchants are making more per sale than ever before.

Looking at a 30-year principal and interest loan, on that $379,000 average, the lowest commission "leading lending institutions" pay is about $1,900. The highest? Almost $26,000.

Although the merchants and probably the MFAA continue to argue otherwise, the conflict of interest commissions create is just as bad as it ever was.

Actually, it's worse.

Then there's the spoken word

Whilst the wordsmith wields written words with near fatal precision, the debt merchants perched behind the counter of your local branch, or the ones that come into your home to be your new best friend have a little more freedom. For these people, the beauty of the spoken word is that it is dynamic, responsive, and difficult to prove.

At the start of this book, you read some shocking facts about one of the more 'significant' actions ASIC has taken against any mortgage broker or lender. The issue of course, was the brokers misleading claims around unbiased advice. These claims were easily proved by ASIC as they were written down, printed out, or posted on the internet. Since then, many merchants, well aware of this precedent, have removed 'unbiased' from their marketing and advertising materials.

> *"Ah, people only know what you tell them, Carl"*
> *from the movie 'Catch me if you can' based on the true story of serial conman Frank Abagnale Jr.*

It's a no-brainer that the written word carries a much higher risk of being caught and the inconvenience of a slap on the wrist from regulators. Most in the industry realised that it's easier to stop publicly advertising 'unbiased advice' than do anything that actually neutralises anti-consumer bias. Especially when the system lenders and brokers have set up has such serious problems.

For the most part, 'unbiased' anything has become a no-no in the written form. However it has not stopped merchants from clever discussions, marketing tools and tricks to create the impression that they are offering unbiased help and are on the borrowers side. They're not.

For example, at the time I researched Mortgage Free, Debt Free, the Aussie website featured a bunch of testimonials from happy customers. These included Lydia, a first homebuyer who borrowed $250,000 in what is undoubtedly the most significant financial decision in her life so far. To the unwitting, Lydia's closing testimony of her experience with Aussie is very reassuring. "They were un-biased with their comparisons and only interested in the best loan to suit my needs".

Although it is impossible to know how Lydia formed this belief, the fact is she has. Yet franchisees and contractors bearing the Aussie moniker receive different commission payments depending on what loan amount, what loan term, which features and which of Aussie's lenders you take. So too does Aussie.

That's different upfront payments as well as different trail commission payments based purely on the question of which of Aussie's lenders wins your business. And the difference is staggering.

According to Aussie's "Finance Broking Agreement and Appointment to Act", Aussie, its franchisees and its contractors can increase upfront commission earnings by almost 300% simply by helping you choose one of their lenders over the other.

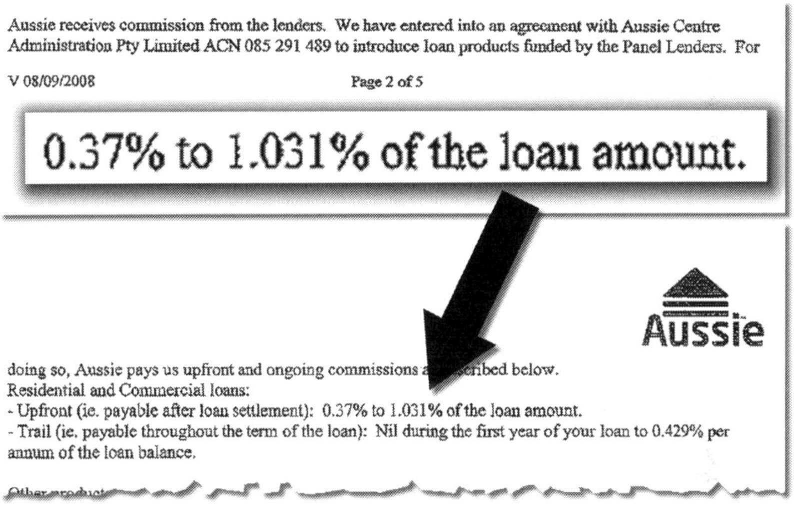
Aussie receives commission from the lenders. We have entered into an agreement with Aussie Centre Administration Pty Limited ACN 085 291 489 to introduce loan products funded by the Panel Lenders. For

V 08/09/2008 Page 2 of 5

doing so, Aussie pays us upfront and ongoing commissions a[illegible]cribed below.
Residential and Commercial loans:
- Upfront (ie. payable after loan settlement): 0.37% to 1.031% of the loan amount.
- Trail (ie. payable throughout the term of the loan): Nil during the first year of your loan to 0.429% per annum of the loan balance.

Of course, it's important to remember that upfront commissions are the smallest slice of the commission pie. Trail commissions are where merchants like Aussie make serious money at your expense. For example, Homeside, a lender on Aussie's panel, offers around 9 times more trail commission than it does in upfront. More again if the broker manages to tweak your term, your loan amount or your features. That's right, the exact same loan, with the same lender and just slightly different features can cost you a lot extra and earn everybody else more profit.

As informative as Aussie's disclosure is, it falls well short of enabling anyone to calculate the real value of commission pressure conflicts in areas where Aussie and any other merchant specifically provides advice to consumers. That's commission pressure suffered by the brokers when giving advice and also by Aussie when selecting its products. Nonetheless, the disclosure appears to meet all legal obligations and the requirements of the MFAA, which only goes to show how low the bar has been set. Even though all of the boxes are ticked, the information you get to inform you of the potential anti-you bias is almost useless.

It is also important to remember that a large slice of Aussie is owned by the Commonwealth Bank and Aussie isn't just a small player in the mortgage broker market. Aussie is a lender, a mortgage broker, an industry influencer, a training ground for new brokers and long standing member of the MFAA.

But wait… there's more

Like quite a few people the world over, I enjoy the odd drop of Australian wine. In particular, I am a huge fan of Shiraz. Although I have enjoyed Shiraz for a little over two decades, I only recently learned that a bottle of wine with a single grape type on the label is known as a varietal. The interesting thing about varietals is they only have to contain 85% of the grape that appears on the label. So in my case, a bottle labelled as Shiraz from a top vineyard, could include up to 15% of Aunty Ruth's home grown roughies, which were rejected by the Sunbeam Sultana factory.

I guess the rule makers set this percentage because they felt that leaving out any more than 15% of what's advertised could be misleading to the consumer or in the very least, a little unfair. Before I learnt about these rules (called the Australian Wine and Brandy Corporation Regulations 1981), I assumed that Shiraz meant 100% Shiraz.

Anyhow, back to your mortgage. For you, Aussie's disclosure that its brokers get a minimum of 0.37% in upfront commission probably went in one eye and out the other. However, it set alarm bells off for me and let me tell you why.

Although a layperson may not notice, the Aussie consumer disclosure does not appear to divulge the full rate of commission paid by the lender to Aussie. At a rough guess, it looks more like 65% - 66% of the commission Aussie is likely to receive from its panel lenders. On realising this, alarm bells rang because:

1. Aussie lists AMP as one of its panel lenders.
2. AMP has a range of products known as Affinity.
3. Affinity products are amongst the most competitive loans AMP offers.
4. AMP pays 0.3% in upfront commission for Affinity.
5. 65% x 0.3% is 0.195%.
6. This is below the minimum 0.37% disclosed by Aussie.

This means that at least one of the following must be true:

A. Aussie tops up the commission from its own pocket.

B. The commission disclosure is wrong.

C. Aussie selects and excludes products available from its lenders range based on commission paid for that loan.

Although I don't have the answer as it relates to AMP, it may become clearer by looking at the big four, which you might recall are the Commonwealth Bank, ANZ, Westpac, and National Australia Bank.

It seems reasonable to expect that brokers such as Aussie would have the big four amongst its lenders, especially given borrowers consistent demand for their products. Turn to Aussies website and you find explanations like "Mortgage Explorer™ compares your needs and preferences with loan features… from our panel of 16 lenders, including the big four banks".

> Mortgage Explorer™ compares your needs and preferences with loan features, interest rates and key fees and charges. It's constantly updated with the latest loans from our panel of 16 lenders, including the big four banks.

In case you didn't know, Mortgage Explorer™ is proprietary loan comparison software that is unique to the Aussie sales team. Early in its life, Mortgage Explorer™ was audited and given a clean bill of health as offering impartial comparisons between different lender options and it is likely that the same statement is as true today as it was back then.

However, ask Aussie the right question and "Mortgage Explorer ™… constantly updated with the latest loans from our panel of 16 lenders, including the big four …" becomes:

"NAB (National Australia Bank) are not included on our Aussie software programme called Mortgage Explorer…"

And there you have it. GIGO.

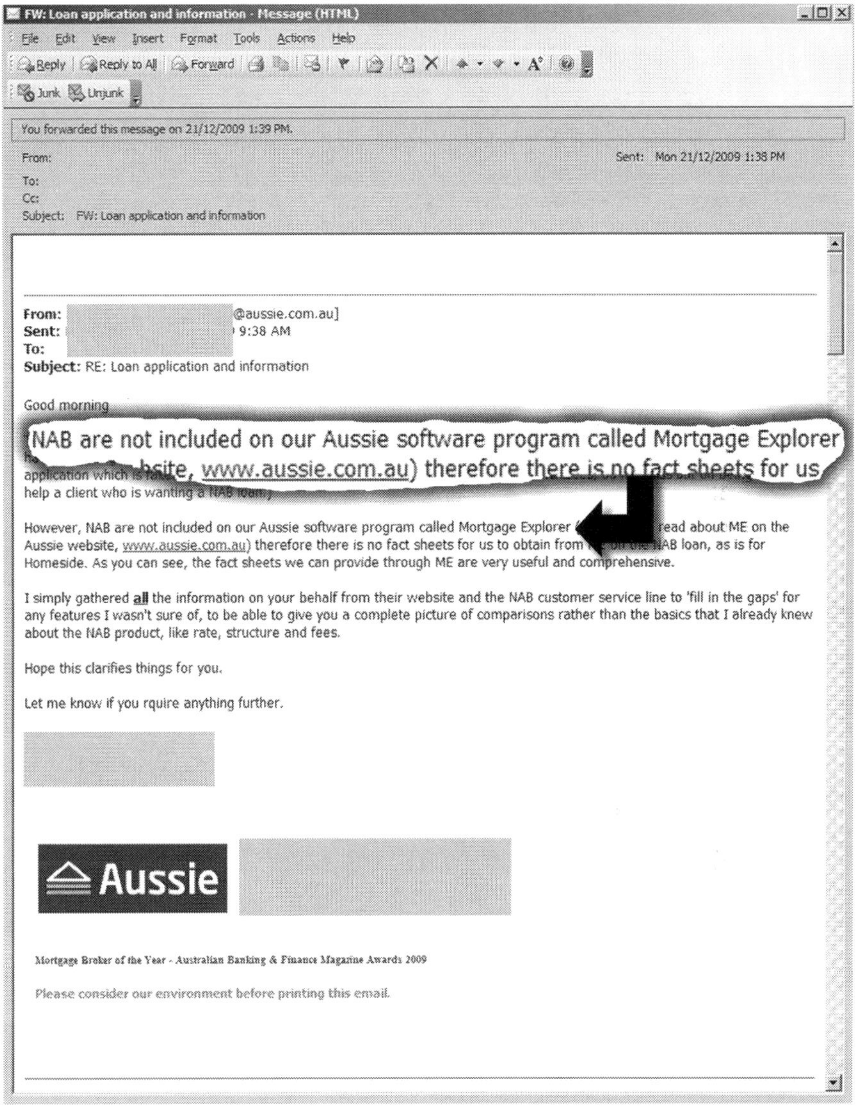

FW: Loan application and information - Message (HTML)

File Edit View Insert Format Tools Actions Help

Reply | Reply to All | Forward

Junk Unjunk

You forwarded this message on 21/12/2009 1:39 PM.

From: Sent: Mon 21/12/2009 1:38 PM
To:
Cc:
Subject: FW: Loan application and information

From: @aussie.com.au]
Sent: 9:38 AM
To:
Subject: RE: Loan application and information

Good morning

NAB are not included on our Aussie software program called Mortgage Explorer
bsite, www.aussie.com.au) therefore there is no fact sheets for us

application which
help a client who is wanting

However, NAB are not included on our Aussie software program called Mortgage Explorer read about ME on the Aussie website, www.aussie.com.au) therefore there is no fact sheets for us to obtain from AB loan, as is for Homeside. As you can see, the fact sheets we can provide through ME are very useful and comprehensive.

I simply gathered **all** the information on your behalf from their website and the NAB customer service line to 'fill in the gaps' for any features I wasn't sure of, to be able to give you a complete picture of comparisons rather than the basics that I already knew about the NAB product, like rate, structure and fees.

Hope this clarifies things for you.

Let me know if you rquire anything further.

Aussie

Mortgage Broker of the Year - Australian Banking & Finance Magazine Awards 2009

Please consider our environment before printing this email.

What most consumers don't realise is National Australia Bank (NAB) has a subsidiary called Homeside. Even though NAB is the lender on the mortgage for Homeside loans, Homeside and the National Australia Bank products are different. Different pricing, different terms and conditions, different credit policies. Different. Unlike Aunty Ruth's home grown roughies, the National Australia Bank products are often more highly regarded than NAB's more limited Homeside range.

Although well heeled lawyers may cleverly argue that Homeside is one of 'the big four', the Homeside range represents quite a bit less than half of the residential mortgage products that National Australia Bank has available.

If Aussie was labelling wine, they probably couldn't call Homeside a 'big four' now, could they?

Interestingly enough, National Australia Bank pays brokers one of the lowest commissions in the market for "NAB" branded loans. These low commission NAB loans are the ones Aussie excludes from its comparison software.

On the other hand, NAB pays the highest commissions in the entire mortgage broker marketplace for its Homeside range. These maximum commission NAB loans are the ones readily compared by Aussie in its Mortgage Explorer software. Meanwhile, the low commission paying loans don't get a look in.

However, this commission thing must be a coincidence because the MFAA tells us "they would not last long in today's competitive environment if they put commission first". Aussie has not just lasted, but has thrived.

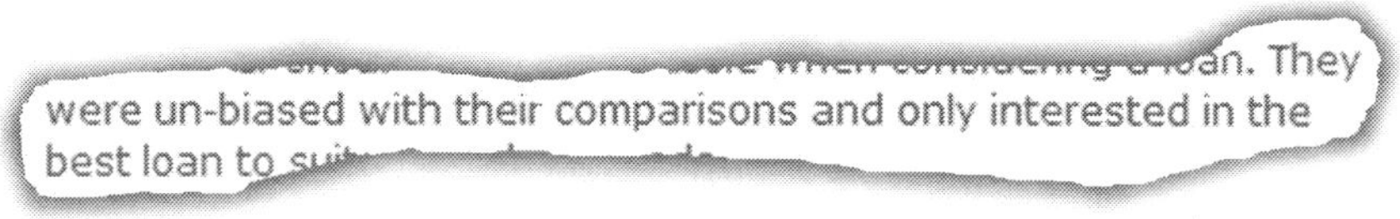
They
were un-biased with their comparisons and only interested in the
best loan to

All this is very curious, however it's where the rubber hits the road that counts. I cannot help but wonder how Lydia the first homebuyér, formed the view that Aussie was 'un-biased with their comparisons and only interested in the best loan to suit me'.

Had Lydia truly received unbiased advice she would probably wind up $30,000 better off. Perhaps more and perhaps even with the exact same loan and lender.

Worse than this, Lydia's misunderstanding is being broadcast to the world as a believable, reliable testimonial of fact. Not just by Lydia, but by Aussie on their website.

While Lydia and others like her are left to foot the bill, I am quietly confident that somewhere, some clever wordsmith will be paid a lot of money to construct an explanation. Then again, it's probably cheaper for Aussie to blame their broker, change the subject and wait until it all just goes away.

Fool's gold

Impartial awards, unbiased advice, independent research groups. You name it, the mortgage industry is rife with brokers, advertising companies, web sites and others claiming to be independent and dangling promises of impartial, simple help to save you time and money.

Back in 1975, Australian band Skyhooks rocketed to the top of the charts with a song called "Ego is not a dirty word". As well as being a chart topping success, the song was a protest against the increasingly popular idea that having an ego was a bad thing. Ego, Skyhooks argued in terms that sometimes still confuse me, has a good side too. It has real benefits. Simply lumping ego into one big 'dirty' bucket ignores its positive attributes.

> *"If you did not have an ego you might not care the way you dressed*
> *If you did not have an ego you'd just be like the rest"*

Decades later and we discover that the rather old fashioned and valuable idea of bias is getting the same, dirty reputation that ego had in 1975. This started when research companies like CANNEX promoted itself as independent. Mortgage brokers claiming they were 'totally unbiased' or they provided 'unbiased home loan advice' quickly followed. Companies that sell advertising to lenders and brokers, brokers who sell borrowers to lenders, and research companies that sell star ratings to lenders can all use the same trick. Like the most convincing sleight of hand, the impartiality and independence ploy consists of two basic principles.

1. That an independent business is not influenced by lenders and;

2. Impartial advice, also free from lender influence, is actually good for you.

So let's take a quick look at what these words actually mean to understand why independent and impartial advice is often not only useless but can also be dangerous to your own best interests.

The Australian Oxford Dictionary offers a number of definitions for the word "independent" with each seeming quite different to the other. To get to the bottom of what 'independent" really means in the context of mortgage help, I turned to people like you and took a street poll. The poll showed that you thought independent meant "not depending on lenders for an opinion or livelihood", with "not belonging to or supported by a lender" running a close second.

However, another definition hardly raised a vote in the street poll. Not surprisingly, it appears to be the one that brokers and research groups rely on to justify their independence. "Self-governing".

So there you have it. Wiggle room. A loophole.

Despite being paid directly by the lenders to endorse their mortgages through ratings, rankings, comments and advice, 'self-governing' businesses can still declare themselves as independent. For the record, 'self-governing' probably has nothing to do with the advice they give you in helping you select either your lender or loan. It's simply that some businesses promote independence to counter your legitimate concerns about the conflicts of interest they suffer. It can really get in the way when they sidle up beside you, whisper in your ear and help you into debt with a lender that pays them to do it.

Now that we have clarified the 'independence' loophole, what of 'impartiality'? Well the same dictionary defines impartial as "treating all rivals or disputants equally". Now let's get that into perspective.

Imagine for a moment you are on trial for a murder you did not commit. I know this is a little extreme (you'll get used to it by the end of the book); however the legal process is where bias and impartiality concepts are played out and tested on a daily basis. The prosecution is biased; they think you did it and are gunning for you. They want you convicted.

Your legal team, if you have one, is also biased. They are on your side and will do everything reasonable to get you off the hook.

The judge however is impartial and to remain impartial must not care whether you did the crime or not, simply that justice is properly served. If you do not hire a defence team who are biased completely in your favour, you are at the mercy of a judge who is indifferent to your innocence and a prosecution that understands the system and is determined to win.

The question is would you hire a legal team to defend you?

If you answered yes, then you understand that impartiality in itself does not protect you nor does it assure you of a favourable outcome. If you answered no, then you might be offended by the old proverb "He who is his own lawyer has a fool for a client".

Just before we move on, let's pervert the legal system for a moment and pretend that your fate is in the hands of "impartial" judges that are paid solely by the prosecution - the people that are out to get you. Provided judges regard themselves as 'self-governed' they would still be able to declare themselves as independent.

Let's stretch that idea out a little and pretend the prosecution will only pay your judge if you are convicted and may even pay the judge a bonus based on monthly conviction rates across all cases. A rational, thinking person could be forgiven for believing your chances of getting a fair hearing or favourable outcome are kind of slim.

As absurd a situation as it may be, by eliminating the critical checks and balances designed to protect all participants, the system takes on striking similarities to another common relationship.

You, as the person with everything to lose, an 'impartial' mortgage broker as the judge that is paid by the prosecution; which is of course the lender whose only interest is to make a profitable sale.

Think about that.

Disclosure Notice:
I am not impartial. I am dedicated to protecting and advancing the interests of you the borrower.

Although the mortgage market is a tricky place to navigate, law is definitely far more complex.

If you do ever find yourself accused of murder or any crime for that matter, I strongly urge you to get the best possible defence team you can afford.

Keep left unless overtaking

In Australia, most states and territories have a law requiring drivers to keep left unless overtaking. Travel along any of our freeways, motorways and highways and you will see the road signs that remind us of the law, our obligation and sometimes, the penalty. However you will also regularly see drivers who idle along in the right hand lane even though they clearly are not overtaking.

Travelling at and sometimes below the speed limit, these otherwise law-abiding people who could be you or someone you know and trust, have a flagrant disregard for this particular law and the impact their behaviour has on those around them. They do this because they know they are unlikely to be caught, even less likely to be seriously penalised and are more concerned with their own personal interests than those around them.

Australia has had road rules, which have applied to drivers since 1909. They prohibit everything from speeding and running red lights through to driving under the influence of alcohol or drugs. These laws, their regulation and driver education have been given ever-increasing attention, with penalties also becoming increasingly harsh. Yet they have done little to reduce the death toll on our roads or kerb anti social driving. The problems are still there. Introducing new laws simply means more laws are broken. It does not fix the problem.

As with driving, many aspects of how lenders and brokers should behave are also enshrined in law and regulation; however this simply does not make you safe. Like the thousands of people behind the wheel who break the law on our roads, there are always lenders and mortgage brokers who just don't take their responsibility seriously.

Then of course, there's those who don't break the law so much as exploit it.

The Six o'clock Swill

Although you are not likely to remember it, six o'clock closing time was introduced at hotels during World War I in response to concerns over our national drinking culture. The laws supported a view that men staying in pubs and drinking heavily until late into the evening posed a serious risk to the family unit, potentially damaging the fabric of society. In other words, closing time laws were created in an attempt to improve public morals and get men home to their families more sober and earlier.

Instead, the early closing time fuelled an hour-long speed drinking session, as men raced to drink as much as possible in the short time between when they finished work at five and when 'last drinks' was called at six o'clock. For better or worse, this binge drinking response has become a part of our nation's history, if not our culture and is immortalised as the "Six o'clock Swill".

Under the new laws, after calling 'last drinks', bartenders were allowed to refill a patron's empty glass one more time. In addition to drinking each beer faster, with shorter breaks in between, drinkers determined to have their fill also realised a loophole. By keeping their empty glasses each time they ordered a fresh beer, they could have several empties refilled once 'last drinks' was called. Bartenders, who were only ever interested in legally selling more beer, adhered to the letter of the law yet still sold multiple beers to each patron after calling 'last drinks'.

It's hard to imagine that this was quite the outcome the lawmakers had planned. Intentions aside, it's what they got.

Comparison Rates... Last drinks Gentlemen

At some stage toward the end of the nineties, consumer advocates and various governments became increasingly concerned at the apparent trickery in use by debt merchants advertising their credit products. This of course included mortgages.

Although the concern was probably across all products, there was a popular, justifiable view that debt merchants were emphasising low introductory rates to get borrowers through the door. These rates were relatively short lived with much higher step up rates hitting the borrower for more than 90% of the loan term. Loans across the board also carried a raft of fees and charges that were not being divulged clearly to the borrower at the point of advertising. Enter the Mandatory Comparison Rate. Although it's not the legal term, I'll call this rate the Advertised Comparison Rate as it's the rate that **must** appear in all advertising.

The intention behind Advertised Comparison Rates, which were introduced in 2002, was to simplify cost comparison of different loan products for the ordinary borrower. i.e. those of us without degrees in accounting and finance.

> *"A comparison rate is a tool to help consumers identify the true cost of a loan.*
>
> *It is a rate which includes both the interest rate and fees and charges relating to a loan, reduced to a single percentage figure. For example, a bank's advertised interest rate may be 5.49% and its comparison rate 6.75%."*
> *www.creditcode.gov.au*

In other words, the Government created Comparison Rates to combat merchants who deliberately mixed in different rates and fees to make their loan difficult to compare with their competitors. The industry term is 'obfuscation', which is to obscure, confuse, bewilder or stupefy - words often used by borrowers attempting to compare loans. Let's just call it gobbledygook. Most, if not all lenders and quite a few brokers like gobbledygook because it makes it easier to sell their loans. This probably explains why they caused the problem in the first place.

So when the lawmakers mandated a standard formula allowing merchants to exclude fees which were 'unascertainable', what followed is kind of obvious (so let me get this right. I can get any glass refilled just once?). The cunning made as much of the loan cost unascertainable as they could. Perhaps worse, the legislation helped them justify the fact they don't need to tell you about that cost until it's all too late. They began legally hiding fees that were once out in the open.

How? Well there are a few different tricks, but the simplest one is to take something like a settlement fee that would once have been a fixed amount, make it variable and call it a disbursement. Because the amount of this 'disbursement' might change based on individual circumstances, it doesn't have to be included in the Advertised Comparison Rate. The same is true for valuation fees and so on.

Clever merchants developed fee and loan structures that meant Advertised Comparison Rates were rendered useless via each and every loophole they could find. By exploiting these loopholes, a surprising number of debt merchants have manipulated the

Advertised Comparison Rate to make their loans appear cheaper than they really are. This however is just one crucial flaw. Others include:

- Advertised Comparison Rates do not consider massive fees, which vary by thousands from lender to lender.

- Variations in loan amounts and/or loan terms can produce radically different real costs that contradict Comparison Rates.

- Advertised Comparison Rates are not available for loan combinations or any loan that includes an evergreen Interest Only facility.

- Advertised Comparison Rates do not include discounts and cashback deals which can radically reduce the real cost of your mortgage.

It is common that loans with lower Advertised Comparison Rates are $20,000, $30,000, or $40,000+ more expensive than loans with higher Comparison Rates even on smaller than average loans.

Nonetheless, if you still believe in Comparison Rates, there are three important things to remember:

1. The debt merchants control the numbers that go into the formula.

2. GIGO.

3. The Six o'clock Swill.

The bottom line is that a loan with a lower Advertised Comparison Rate may cost you more. Although it will always be challenging for an untrained person without the right tools to rank different mortgages, there is an answer. It's called Total Individual Cost (TIC) and it allows you to compare between different loan products and different mixes of products more reliably. Sit tight, we'll learn where to get the right tools and how to do it soon.

Quietly bending responsible lending

Of course not all laws require loopholes. Some of them are so floppy that they are difficult to define, let alone enforce. By floppy I mean that people (clever lenders, lawyers, politicians, etc.) can flip them or flop them in whatever direction they want.

For example, although 'responsible lending' is enshrined in a law designed to protect you the consumer, a fairly basic question remains unanswered. What exactly passes as responsible?

To answer that question, let's take a look at just one lending practice that seems to count as responsible lending. I say that it seems to count, because quite a few lenders do it including the majors and nobody seems to bat an eyelid. Yet this practice poses a very high risk to your financial and probably emotional health as well as that of your loved ones. As you read this, please try to remember that responsible lending is a legal obligation placed on lenders and one that is supposed to protect you.

Genworth Financial describes itself as the 'leading provider of Lenders Mortgage Insurance (LMI)'. I'll explain more about that later, but for now it suffices to say that LMI is an insurance policy that protects the lender as your borrowing becomes increasingly risky.

In other words, LMI allows merchants to support risky borrowing provided the lender can still see a chance of a tidy, legal profit and the insurer is willing to accept the risk. Although you may experience complete financial devastation thanks to LMI, the lenders profits are nice and safe because their risk of any fallout from your bad fortune is protected by an insurance policy.

Like all insurance, the higher the risk, the higher the fee; however there is a point where the risk is so high, insurance is simply unavailable. This happens when insurers think they will spend more money on claims than they could hope to collect in fees. These are known as bad or extreme risks. So it makes sense that a professional insurer understands the difference between a good risk and a bad one. If they didn't they would eventually go broke.

As Genworth boasts that it has 'insured over $300 billion of residential mortgages since 1965' you can be pretty confident that they are experts at avoiding bad risks. Genworths' rule book states that 'The "Loan to Value Ratio" (LVR) is one of the major elements of risk and is one of the vital considerations of any LMI proposal".

The maximum risk Genworth is willing to accept under any circumstances is an LVR of 95% and quite a bit less in many cases. In other words, any LVR above 95% is simply too risky and is uninsurable with this massive business which makes its profit by choosing acceptable risks.

Yet quite a few lenders, including the big 4 will lend 100% and in some cases, up to 110% of the purchase price of a property. They do this by suggesting that borrowers could approach a family member to guarantee the loan and tying that family member's property into the loan as well.

You might think that this sounds like a great idea, because you get out of having to save a solid deposit yourself and you can also avoid a big fat mortgage insurance premium. However in doing so, your family becomes your lenders mortgage insurer. People that love you and who are completely inexperienced in gauging this type of risk are asked to insure the bank, (that's right, the bank, not you), against the chance of a financial disaster. Remember, that is the very same risk the lender and their highly experienced, highly profitable, highly professional insurer will not touch for any amount of money. Think about that.

There is no doubt that lenders mortgage insurance has become a necessary evil due to skyrocketing property prices. However it's hard to grasp that asking ordinary every day people who are emotionally attached to the borrower to accept a risk that has been rejected by professional risk assessors could ever be considered as 'responsible'.

Legal, sure. Responsible? Hardly.

Up yours coppa

Setting aside whether a law is a good one or a bad one, for it to work it must be well policed. If a law exists to protect you, it should be enforced. I sat for quite some time trying to decide what to call this section and was torn between "Up yours coppa" and "They're never around when you need one". If you still have a scrap of confidence that regulation protects you or you still have some vague belief in Advertised Comparison Rates, consider this.

The legislation mandating Comparison Rates is very wordy, however there are some fairly straight forward bits explaining when Comparison Rates must be shown. Now I did say 'fairly straight forward" so at first glance it might be as clear as mud, but let's work through it one step at a time. It won't take long, it's simpler than it might first appear and it is very important.

As far as I can tell, the legislation says a Comparison Rate must be quoted whenever an interest rate for every day mortgages is advertised to consumers. This is explained in the law like this:

'146A Object of Part

'**(1)** The object of this Part is to assist consumers to identify the true cost of credit offered by credit providers.

'**(2)** In order to achieve that object, this Part—

(a) makes it mandatory for credit providers to include the comparison rate in advertisements for consumer credit (other than under continuing credit contracts) if an interest rate is advertised; and

So according to 2(a) if you are advertising interest rates, you must include a comparison rate. The next natural question is "what is an 'advertisement for consumer credit'?" The act explains it as:

"credit advertisement" means an advertisement in any form or medium that states or implies that credit is available, but (for the avoidance of doubt) does not include—

(a) notices or other documents required or authorised to be given under this Code; or

(b) a publication that only lists reference rates.

As you can see, the only time an interest rate is not included as an advertisement is when it appears in legal mumbo jumbo that relates to the law itself or a publication which is simply a list of 'reference rates' (what the?). This sent me on the hunt for a definition of 'reference rates' as it is not contained in the legislation itself, so I contacted Ian Clyde.

Ian is the Assistant General Manager for Consumer Policy & Programs at Consumer Affairs Victoria. Putting aside his rather massive job title, he is THE man to ask questions about Comparison Rates.

When I asked Ian what reference rates are, he replied telling me the official view of what a reference rate isn't. This is what he wrote. "The expectation is that the reference rate would not, itself, be a rate available to the public."

According to Ian then, a reference rate would not be one you would see except if you stumbled across internal documentation used by the merchants themselves. At all other times, you should see a Comparison Rate because it counts as advertising.

So now we have that out of the way, what if a merchant only wants to advertise one rate to make it nice and simple for you to choose? The act explains it like this:

> **'146E Comparison rate mandatory in advertisements containing annual percentage rate**
>
> '(**1**) A credit advertisement must contain the relevant comparison rate in accordance with this Part if it contains an annual percentage rate.
>
> '(**2**) A credit advertisement may contain the relevant comparison rate in accordance with this Part even if it does not contain an annual percentage rate.

In other words, if you the public see an interest rate in an everyday public space, it should BE the Comparison Rate or be accompanied by the Comparison Rate. You should also see that silly WARNING to remind you the Advertised Comparison Rate wouldn't ever actually apply to your loan. That's why, whenever you get interest rate printouts from Commonwealth Bank, NAB, ANZ, Westpac and a host of other lenders, you also see that pesky other rate with the asterisk, the Advertised Comparison Rate.

Now when I generalise about a host of other lenders, I do not include St George or others like them as these businesses appear to see their obligations to you quite differently.

For some time now, lenders including St George have opted to readily advertise only one rate for each loan at their web site. And it's not the Comparison Rate.

A snapshot of the interest rates on the St George website appears on the next page without a single Comparison Rate in sight. For the record, the Advertised Comparison Rate for the highlighted loan at St George's web site is closer to 8.00% rather than the 7.10% St George is advertising. My guess is that 7.10% is more likely to get more consumers interested in St George though.

Now to be fair to St George, you can actually GET to the Advertised Comparison Rate, in fact you can get to dozens of them. You just need know that there is a link off the page outside of the visible window that St George pops up (the window NEVER opens with the button visible). You then need to scroll to the bottom of this page click a link that reads 'Comparison Rates'; wait for another web page to appear; "Select a schedule type"; click View/Print Schedule (whatever that means); wait for another web page to open; then find the loan that interests you in yet another list. Of course it would probably be a lot more visible to consumers if the Advertised Comparison Rate appeared in the whopping blank space next to the other interest rate now wouldn't it?

Oh, and there is that other thing, 146I (2) of the legislation states 'A comparison rate in any credit advertisement must not be less prominent than any annual percentage rate stated in the advertisement'.

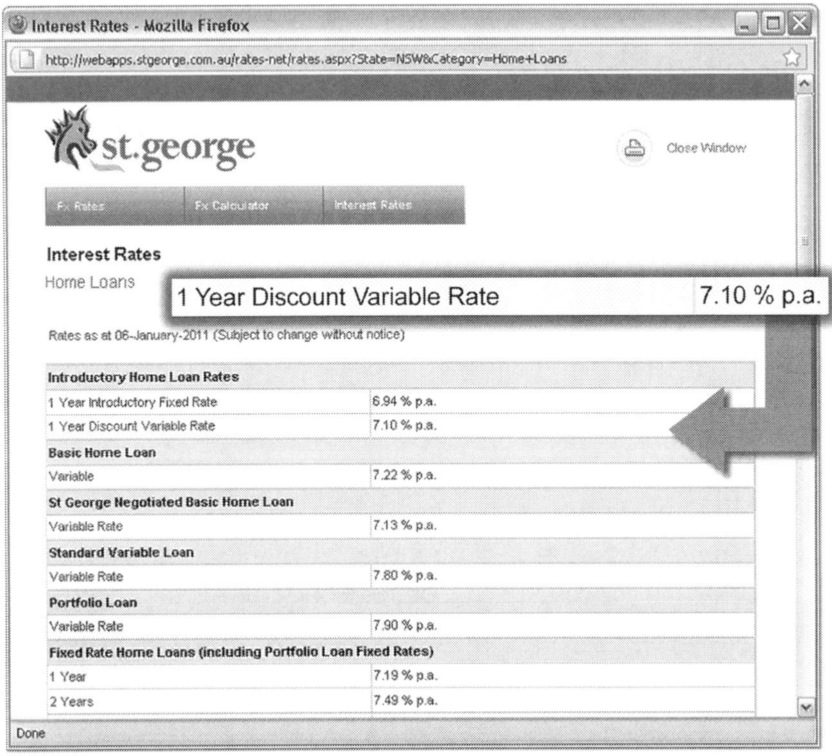
Interest Rates - Mozilla Firefox

http://webapps.stgeorge.com.au/rates-net/rates.aspx?State=NSW&Category=Home+Loans

st.george

Close Window

Fx Rates | Fx Calculator | Interest Rates

Interest Rates

Home Loans

1 Year Discount Variable Rate 7.10 % p.a.

Rates as at 06-January-2011 (Subject to change without notice)

Introductory Home Loan Rates	
1 Year Introductory Fixed Rate	6.94 % p.a.
1 Year Discount Variable Rate	7.10 % p.a.
Basic Home Loan	
Variable	7.22 % p.a.
St George Negotiated Basic Home Loan	
Variable Rate	7.13 % p.a.
Standard Variable Loan	
Variable Rate	7.80 % p.a.
Portfolio Loan	
Variable Rate	7.90 % p.a.
Fixed Rate Home Loans (including Portfolio Loan Fixed Rates)	
1 Year	7.19 % p.a.
2 Years	7.49 % p.a.

Done

How is it that a lender as high profiled as St George gets away with hiding Comparison Rates if credit legislation supposed to protect you really works? Of course they are not the only ones that do it and Comparison Rates don't really help you, but that's not the point.

Regardless of whether the St George approach is legal or otherwise, according to Ian, the spirit of the law requires the Comparison Rate to be clearly shown *with* any other interest rate in order to be fair to consumers. Yet St George clearly rejects that proposition. What's more, they have done this in full view of Westpac as owners of St George; the MFAA, which has St George as a member; and in full view of the Regulators who are responsible for the law that is supposed to protect you.

The point is that if nobody is enforcing something as simple as whether Comparison Rates are properly included in advertising, you can be pretty confident that no one is down in the nitty gritty ensuring they are being calculated correctly…GIGO.

I hope that by now, the message is reaching you loud and clear. There is never a police officer around when you need one. Besides this book and a smattering of borrowers agents scattered around the country, you dear reader, are on your own.

Good debt. Bad debt.

You may have heard a rumour that there's 'good debt' and there's 'bad debt'. It's a line trotted out by people selling a property, a loan or a line, then repeated by those not taking the time to think about it. In the middle of 2009, our political leaders introduced a new term, 'necessary debt'. The truth is debt comes in two types. Manageable debt and terrible debt. Neither of these is inherently good.

Manageable debt is debt you can manage (I can almost hear you groan from here). Managing your mortgage could mean anything from being ahead in your mortgage repayments through to being comfortable with your ability to make repayments. Obviously, the former is better than the latter.

Terrible debt is debt that ranges from being vaguely concerned about future rate rises, right through to finding yourself in a situation where you struggle to, or cannot make a repayment on one debt or another.

Most people with terrible debt don't start out that way nor do they have a burning desire to get into terrible debt. Instead, they meander there aimlessly through a series of poorly informed and thought out decisions. In fact, the most common answer I hear when I ask borrowers how they got into terrible debt is "I don't know". Not long after that, the conversation flows into a long list of 'necessary purchases' that wound up being not so necessary after all, a list of credit cards with ridiculous credit limits and interest free deals and so on.

When you have debt, you have less control over the money you have to do the things you either need to or want to because you can't control your interest cost. This means you don't control your repayments. In fact the larger your debt is, the less control you have over your money and the harder the debt will be to repay. Larger debt also means more compromise on how you live and creates an increased risk that you will run into trouble.

> *"That's the bitchin' part about it! It don't matter! If you can't afford it, F@#!%ING FINANCE IT!"*
> *from the movie Ruthless People, 1986*

A now failed investor spruiking the wonders of negative gearing as a "good debt' investment strategy once said to me 'it is better to pay interest, than it is to pay tax'. This idea might have instant appeal because most of us hate paying taxes; however, it only considers part of the picture. If you are making a loss or just breaking even, it really doesn't matter if you are throwing your money at the taxman or a lender does it? You are still shelling out your hard earned cash to other people. Perhaps what he really meant to say is there are good investments and bad investments. Some are worth buying; some are not. Debt is a vehicle some people use to acquire them.

Whilst debt may be helpful in purchasing large assets that would simply be too difficult for you to buy with savings, debt is otherwise bad. Taking on any new debt should always be considered carefully and once you have debt, it should be eliminated as soon as possible.

> *"A man in debt is so far a slave."*
> *Ralph Waldo Emerson 1803-1882*

Although you may never wind up with terrible debt (follow the ideas in Mortgage Free, Debt Free carefully and you definitely won't), even manageable debt costs you thousands more than it would if you are educated, committed and energised about getting rid of it. So labelling any debt as "good" is a little stupid.

Objects in mirror are closer than they appear

The very first time I threw my leg over a Harley Davidson, I noticed a message etched into the mirror that read, "Objects in mirror are closer than they appear". It was a couple of decades back and convex mirrors, which up until then were only seen in fun parks, had just started to appear on imported vehicles. These mirrors were introduced as a safety measure delivering a wider, yet slightly weirder view of the road. The wider view improved visibility with one unfortunate side effect. The magnification that made the wider view possible also made things smaller, so the car, which appears to be way off in the distance, could actually be just a metre or two from the back of your head.

Perhaps it's because I'm a keen photographer that the warning struck me as odd. To me, it was common sense that a convex mirror changed the scale and depth of the reflections. I then remembered that common sense is not exactly common, as we don't all share the same experience or knowledge. In the case of the convex mirror, things aren't exactly how they appear and this can catch out the otherwise sensible motorist with devastating results. The same holds true for the mother of all debt, your mortgage. It looms, like a Mack Truck in your convex mirror as you hurtle down the financial highway in your tiny little fuel efficient tin can. Things that may seem small and irrelevant are often big and dangerous. If you don't understand what you are looking at, you can make serious mistakes with consequences ranging from costly to devastating. Not checking your mirrors doesn't make you any safer either.

Let's take a quick look at one of the two dozen or so influencers of the cost and manageability of your mortgage, the humble loan term. If your loan repayment seems too high, extending the loan term to reduce monthly costs is a common remedy.

So what happens if you bite off a 25% increase in your loan term? Right now, seeing it written like that makes this decision seem like a big one involving a big number and it is. However many borrowers take that 25% stretch without batting an eyelid simply by choosing a 25 year loan term instead of the once common 20 years. In fact, most of today's borrowers go much further by taking their mortgage over 30 years and in extreme cases 40.

Anyhow, let's get back to 'stretching' your mortgage a mere 5 years from 20 years to 25.

What do you expect will happen to your repayment? What do you expect this will do to your interest costs? Common sense would have many thinking that repayments reduce by say 25% and interest costs might increase by 25%. If you think this sounds about right, you just changed lanes in front of that Mack truck. Nothing could be further from the truth.

A 20-year loan, which has a minimum weekly repayment of $685, will cost you a total of $333,691 in interest. Increase the loan term by 25% and those payments reduce by less than 9% - well below the reduction that many borrowers expect.

However, on the Mack truck side of the equation, interest blows out to a whopping $434,851 some $101,000 more than the shorter, traditional term - an increase of more than 30%. Don't forget, you still have to repay the debt too.

You get a mild lower repayment 'benefit' whilst your merchant gets a wild higher income benefit. The money that slips quietly from your pocket goes straight into theirs.

Term	Weekly Payment	Payment Reduces	Interest Paid	Interest Increases
20 years	$685	-	$333,691	-
25 years	$626	8.64%	$434,851	30.32%

Your repayment falls by just $59 a week, costing you over $101,000 extra in interest when you increase your loan term by just 5 years!

This happens because interest is calculated on a compound basis, whereas we often think in simple interest terms and they are radically different concepts. Even if you don't understand the math behind this, it's critical that you understand that even small numbers have a very big impact over time. This can work for you or, as it does for most borrowers, can work in favour of the merchant that helps you choose and 'structure' your loan. But it can't do both.

It's much smarter and quite simple to turn the equation around to work in your favour. Keep reading. Make sure you get the right loan. Cut out a coffee a day from the local café and make your own lunch. Use that money to keep your loan term down and get debt free faster.

Nothing up my sleeve... presto

Misdirection is a favourite tool for magicians; they have been using it for years. Your eye is hypnotically drawn to their left hand waving a brightly coloured scarf, while the magicians right hand sneaks into a hidden pocket to grab a coin that soon appears as if from nowhere.

The scarf is known in the magic trade as a prop, because it "props up" the overall illusion. The prop and the slightly exaggerated gestures that draw your attention are deliberately designed to guide you to where the magician wants you to look, or more commonly, to keep you from looking where the magician does not want you to look.

If you want to figure out what's really going on, you need to look at the hand that is not frantically waving in the air. Of course, it's not always a scarf, sometimes it's a scantily clad assistant, a clown, a magic wand or just about anything else you can imagine. It just comes down to how the magician thinks they can successfully capture and hold the attention of the audience and through this, create the illusion.

Like magicians, the merchants have been making carefully choreographed moves and waving brightly coloured scarves to capture business for years. In recent times, increased competition has created new pressure on lenders to find new props to capture your attention. All of them are designed to trigger your curiosity or capture your confidence.

From my perspective, some of them seem less honest than others; although I have trouble calling any of them particularly fair.

The usual suspects that you are likely to be familiar with include:

- ✗ No application fee.
- ✗ Apply now, our variable rate is a low x.xx%.
- ✗ No ongoing fees.
- ✗ Low comparison rate.
- ✗ Award winning loans.
- ✗ Free holidays, plasma, or other gimmicks.
- ✗ Massive savings on the big bank's standard variable.
- ✗ We're not like the big banks.
- ✗ Look! Five star rating.
- ✗ We're a big bank, so you're safe with us.

Of course, there are plenty more and they are all equally hokey examples of misdirection. These simple messages may well be true, but they are really cleverly designed by marketing teams to help one merchant or the other stand out from the crowd and distract you from the stuff you really should be focussed on.

Ignore the hype. It never lasts, but the pain of misdirection might go on for years.

It's life Jim, but not as we know it

Okay, if you're not an avid Star Trek fan (I'm not, but respect peoples right to be) and if you can't remember the pop music of the late eighties, or deliberately choose to forget it, then you may not be familiar with this line. However these words were first uttered by Mr Spock when explaining to Captain Kirk that life has more than one definition. The same is true for many words in the English language including and especially the different catches, fees and features of different mortgage options available today.

I was only recently researching variable rate mortgage products and had arrived at a shortlist of four loans from four different lenders. Although features weren't the primary focus of this research, one of these loans included a fully transactional, 100% Offset Account.

Three of the loans readily identified themselves as Basic Variables, while the fourth included the word 'Pro' in its name.

If asked to guess which loan had the offset account on a first impression, I would have said the 'Pro'. If you thought differently, then well done, but for me, something inside my head automatically connected the word 'pro' with the term 'pro pack' as in professional pack. This created an impression of a top of the line, professional loan, or at least something more sophisticated than a basic loan. However when I dug deeper into the marketing literature, a red light went on and sirens sounded.

So I picked up the phone and called the lender. When I asked whether the 'Pro' included an offset account, the lender replied "It has a redraw account that you can put money in and take it back out".

Ahhh, right. So that would be a 'no'. Although the lender offered an arguably true, cleverly crafted statement, they did not answer the actual question. The 'Pro' did not have an offset account, full stop. It was a basic loan with a debit card that allowed extra payments and included a redraw facility.

Ironically, the loan with a real life name of 'Basic Variable' was the only loan with a fully transactional, 100% Offset account. Ironic because the 'Pro' doesn't have one, yet the 'Basic' does. Who would have thought?

Without becoming buried in a litany of examples, it suffices to say that one lender's offset may be radically different to another's. One lender may claim to have no application fees, yet still charge several thousand dollars more to 'establish' your loan than a lender that advertises application fees and so on. But it doesn't stop there.

> *"Try not to confuse confidence with delusion."*
> *Seth Godin*

The marketing and legal departments of the merchants work furiously to create confusion so they can then provide you with a simple, good value rescue package that looks better than the next guy's. However that doesn't mean you should fall for the delusion that a mortgage is a mortgage, redraw is redraw, a fixed rate is a fixed rate and so on. Because they aren't.

Falsies

After years of crunching numbers, pressing lenders for real information, wading through piles of advertising and choking down truckloads of marketing puffery, I can tell you that it's not just things you find hard to believe that you should question. Things you find easy to believe should be put to the test as well as they are just as likely to send you up the proverbial creek without a paddle.

There are quite a few myths doing the rounds that are completely believable and equally wrong. You know, the things that slip past our inbuilt lie detectors because they sound right, make sense, or seem or look real. But they are still wrong. In fact there are enough of these falsies out there that I could write a whole book just about them. Hang on, perhaps someone already has and it's probably called the mortgage sales guide for merchants.

Here's some that you might have heard or read:

Bells and Whistles cost more.

I've got to start out by confessing that I don't even know what the heck a mortgage bell or whistle is, let alone what they might be used for.

However if you think bells and whistles are things like an offset account, portability or redraw, then you can safely say they don't cost any extra for the average borrower. By the time you finish reading Mortgage Free, Debt Free you will be able to get a loan with the bells and whistles for less than the price of one without them. Ding Ding.

If it sounds too good to be true it probably is.

Probably, but not definitely. If it sounds too good to be true yet the idea interests you, it's worth taking the time to understand it. If you understand it and it still sounds good, get a qualified, professional opinion. If it still sounds good, go for it.

You can get a better deal going direct.

This <u>might</u> be true if your ONLY option is to deal with the lender directly to get the loan you must have or the one that you think is the absolute best. However if the lender is available via a mortgage broker, then you will always get a better deal using the right broker due to a number of factors ranging from buying power through to cashback deals. Even with the right one, taking any merchant's advice on features, lenders or loan options before reading Mortgage Free, Debt Free cover to cover is just plain silly.

Paying fortnightly can save you thousands.

Paying extra saves thousands, paying fortnightly does not.

Award winning mortgages are better.

Most mortgage awards are judged by people on tight deadlines looking at way too many products and who know little about loans and even less about you. Nevertheless an award or a rating can make you feel better while you are making a bad choice. So I guess this one is kind of true.

A Five Star Loan is the best.

For star rating systems like Canstar CANNEX, if lenders don't pay to have their loans rated, they don't get rated. That means a loan with no rating can easily beat one with five stars on value, price, features, flexibility and anything else that might be important to you. You can also bet that their rating methods, like comparison rates will never apply to you. This means they might award it five stars, when it's only worth two to you.

If that isn't enough to convince you to ignore star ratings handed out by these types of companies, simply remember that your mortgage will last you for years, yet a loan with a five star rating today, might be four stars tomorrow or even three stars only a few months down the track.

Brokers make most of their commission upfront.

Although brokers prefer not to talk about it, trail commission is where the real money is. Upfront may be 0.60%, but a trail of 0.25% p.a. that steps up over time completely dwarfs it. Ask your broker to write down the dollar amount for each of them if you still doubt me.

A mortgage is a mortgage, there's not much in it.

Ummm. No. If you don't already know about The Free Money Strategy, have never heard of the Savings Plan, then you are already behind the eight ball. When it comes to saving money and clearing your debt quickly, the mortgage you have, or may be about to take, could be like trying to win Bathurst in a car you bought from Mr Bean.

If you still believe any of these, drop me a line, I've got a great block of land to sell on a perfect little sun drenched island.

It's got 360 degree water views and great development potential. Of course, it's not zoned for building at the moment and swamps may be prone to flooding, but at $450,000, it's a steal.

If I've still got it when my private jet comes back from its service we'll fly on over and take a look. You'll love it.

That's if it's still for sale. I've knocked twenty grand off the price for a strictly limited time and at just $430,000, it will sell at any tick of the clock.

If you want to grab yourself a bargain, don't wait.

Act now.

Mutual Shmutual

For years credit unions and building societies, let's call them 'the mutuals' have screamed that they offer a better deal for borrowers because they are not for profit. But is that really true?

Not for profit is sentimentally a nice idea, but governments, including my local council are all non profit. That doesn't mean they offer good value on price, service or just about anything. Quite frankly, they are all a bit of a disappointment in many aspects that are really important to me and fairly mundane for everything else.

The reality is whether you take your loan with a profit driven bank or one of the mutuals, your loan still costs you money. The money you spend on that loan still goes back to a business where they do with it what they want.

The only certain difference between the mutuals and profit driven banks is that part of the money you spend with a profit driven bank goes out to the shareholders, but most of it doesn't.

When it comes to your mortgage, it is important to find the best deal for <u>you</u>. Whether your lender turns a profit or not has nothing to do with whether your loan will cost you less or work any better.

“If you would be wealthy, think of saving as well as getting.”

Benjamin Franklin

Revision: Clearing the air

Congratulations, you are on the way. You should now have a firm understanding that:

- ✓ Lenders Sell.
- ✓ Mortgage Brokers Sell.
- ✓ Lenders pay Mortgage Brokers to Sell.
- ✓ It's the things they don't tell you that cost you.
- ✓ Comparison Rates mean very little.
- ✓ The laws to protect you are as useful as udders on a bull.
- ✓ There's never a cop around when you need one.
- ✓ Things aren't always what they seem.
- ✓ Compound interest can really work against you.
- ✓ Businesses paid directly by lenders to endorse products can still promote themselves as independent.
- ✓ The only person you should trust is you and the people you have paid to protect you.

Part II: How to Beat the Banks and the Brokers

"To win the game, you need to understand the rules"
Michael Lee

Now that we've cleared the air, it's time to get on with learning how to beat the banks and the brokers by making better choices.

At the heart of every smart decision there is a set of rules, a plan that fits those rules and the action required to implement your plan. Follow these rules, make your plan, and take action. To Beat the Banks and the Brokers you need to:

1. Avoid common costly mistakes.

2. Get the most effective mortgage for your situation.

3. Squeeze what you can out of it right up to the day you get rid of it.

STEP 1

Avoid common, costly mistakes

"A danger foreseen is half avoided"
Unknown

Rather than blindly following a set of rules, smart people prefer to understand the principles behind them. So let's take a close look at common, costly mistakes to help us understand the most important principles that help you to avoid them. Costly might be anything from ten thousand dollars disappearing down the drain unnoticed, to financial and emotional devastation.

Most borrowers make at least two of these costly mistakes.

Smart borrowers don't make any.

Brand loyalty is where you favour a certain brand because you, your father, mother, brother, sister, partner or mate have been using them for years.

It's a great way to pay more, get less and might be fine when buying chocolate. When it comes to something as costly as your mortgage it's nuts.

Get a quote from your favourite lenders. If they won't offer you the best deal, then your loyalty is a one way street – and you're the one paying the cab fare.

Thinking like a teenager

A few decades back when I was in Year 9, I studied economics. When I say studied, what I really mean is that I spent time in a classroom where the teacher was teaching economics. My teacher was a tiny lady called Mrs Reid and when I say tiny, she really was. At that age I was only five foot four in the old money and Mrs Reid barely came up to my shoulder. She had a thinning but well dyed head of curly brown hair and her nickname was Granny Reid. Not because she liked green apples, merely because she seemed like she was 150 years old.

When Granny Reid became exasperated, which was every fifteen minutes or so, she would sort of clear her mind and probably her throat by starting every sentence with "Er, er".

It seems that at least once a class, every class, I would hear Granny Reid's "Er, er" warm up before she would say "Know it, you've done it, have you Mr Lee?"

At 15, I was cocky. I thought the answer to this question was yes. I thought I knew a lot and at least enough to get by. I thought that I could never get it that wrong. Ironically, I couldn't have been more wrong just by thinking that I couldn't get it wrong. It was Granny Reid who helped me discover it, acknowledge it and do something about it.

Granny Reid is forever etched in my mind for what she drummed into me and I now refer to her as Granny with a fondness, rather than the ignorance of a teenager. I didn't know it and I hadn't done it. Don't think like a teenager and definitely don't think like me as a teenager.

The number one way to cost yourself thousands and delay your arrival at financial freedom is to think that nothing you learn in Mortgage Free, Debt Free could happen to you.

How much you CAN borrow
is usually more than
how much you SHOULD borrow

Swallowing the standard

Even amongst the swirling masses of loans, lenders features and interest rates, there is one label that shines like some sort of beacon in the dark. The Standard Variable Rate. Like bugs to a porch light in the middle of a hot summers night, it mysteriously draws two types of people; clever wordsmiths working in the marketing departments of the debt merchants and their victims.

Standard variable, as with many things mortgage, is often quite misunderstood and the price of getting it wrong can be significant. There are two mistakes commonly involving standard variable. Both of these hoodwink consumers into a false sense of savings.

The first is where clever lenders brazenly advertise savings using comparisons of their 'super sharp rate' against their competitor's standard variable, with 'the big banks standard variable' being a popular target.

Institution	Variable Rate (p.a.)	Comp Rate# (p.a.)	Fees
myrate ($600k+)	6.99%	6.99%	$0*
myrate ($100k+)	7.03%	7.03%	$0*
Commonwealth	7.81%	7.94%	$600
ANZ	7.80%	7.90%	$600
Westpac	7.86%	7.99%	$600
St. George	7.80%	7.96%	$700

This myrate advertisement is typical of comparisons small lenders make with the 'big banks' Standard Variable. You will soon learn how to get a far better deal with any of myrate's listed competitors than you can with myrate.

The second is where merchants promote discounts of X% off standard variable. So what is the Standard Variable Rate and what exactly does it mean to you?

The bit that confuses most people is the word 'standard'. According to the Australian Oxford Dictionary, a standard is "a measure serving as a basis by which others can be compared". If you find yourself re-reading that definition, don't worry, I did too. It just says that a 'standard' is a basis for comparison. So when you see one lender comparing their rate against another's standard variable rate it should be kosher right? Wrong. The fact that the dictionary can't clear this up for us shows just why clever marketing departments and probably the legal guys protecting the merchants love the standard variable rate so much.

In reality, a Standard Variable Rate is little more than a reference rate that you will almost never actually pay. The most important things to understand are:

1. Each lender has its own standard variable rate.

2. A standard variable rate is usually a 'fully loaded' reference rate, rather than one you will actually pay.

3. Lenders use their standard variable rate as a benchmark to set the interest rates for their own variable rate products.

4. Everybody should be paying less than their lender's standard variable rate.

5. Comparing any rate against any 'standard variable rate' is a marketing trick that will hurt not help you.

Oh, and getting X% off the standard variable rate is also another marketing trick. This classic misdirection gets consumers thinking about the size of the discount and the apparent generosity/skill of the merchant rather than the actual cost of their loan. Set aside the misdirection and it's a no brainer that you can get a big discount off a high price, yet still save more with a smaller discount off a lower price. Comparing discounts off the standard variable rate between different lenders has no real value to you as a borrower, so don't do it.

By the way, if you ever find yourself actually paying the standard variable rate, make sure you dust this book off before you whack yourself on the forehead with it a few times.

Rushing in

No matter what your reason for needing a new mortgage, you are likely to be either excited or stressed when it is time to get things moving. Whether you are clearing old debts or racing to get your new property settled on time, you can be forgiven for wanting it over and done with as soon as possible.

Merchants keen to pedal their wares understand that getting an emotional commitment from a buyer is a powerful guarantee of a sale. Also knowing that many borrowers are anxious about taking out a mortgage, merchants use a number of perfectly legal and very clever methods to get that commitment from you. These can range from simple verbal cues and reassurances to advertising bearing promises of super fast approvals or offers of a special discounted rate, fee waiver or other incentive for 'a strictly limited time'.

"For fools rush in where angels fear to tread"
Alexander Pope (21 May 1688 – 30 May 1744)

However rushing in to the wrong mortgage can quickly become far more costly than missing out on the right one boasting a limited time offer, especially when many of these deals may be extended anyway. Rushing in can also be far more costly than pressing tightly against a settlement deadline which a good broker, borrowers agent or conveyancer should be able to negotiate away for you anyway.

While writing Mortgage Free, Debt Free, I found a wonderful example of the 'limited time only' marketing technique in use at Resi's web site.

If you landed there as I did, you could be forgiven for feeling either heightened anxiety or excitement about getting things rolling quickly. Resi's home page urged "Hurry limited time only! Save up to $700 with no fees". This instruction to hurry is reinforced with regular calls to action encouraging you to "Enquire online" and was also bolstered with reassuring testimonials that everything will be okay and various 'feel good' awards.

Although the Resi loan might be the right one for you, giving in to their prompts to 'Hurry' for such a massive financial decision is just plain silly.

The simple fact is that when you hurry, you are likely to miss things and missing things can be very costly indeed. While it's true that $700 might go some way to covering costs like conveyancing or duties, choosing a mortgage is a decision that will end up costing you several hundred thousand dollars. A once off $700 saving is probably not that important when a small oversight involving such a big debt could wipe out that saving in a heartbeat.

Of course if that was $700 a year, it might be a different story, although you should *still* take your time to make sure you are getting the right mortgage and that the annual saving is genuine.

You should also remember that any 'special' offer is limited only by a merchants desire to win your business and because of this, these offers can be extended. It's worth pointing out that Resi's 'limited offer' including the snapshot of Resi's web site is from December 2009. This is quite a few months after the expiry of a strikingly similar offer promising a saving of up to $700 in September that same year. For the record, Resi was advertising a 'No upfront fees - Limited offer' in October too. And the beat goes on.

However the insistence that you hurry isn't the exclusive domain of just one merchant. A year later and one of the big banks seems to agree with Resi that it is a good idea to urge you to rush on in with a "Hurry limited time only" Fixed Rate deal.

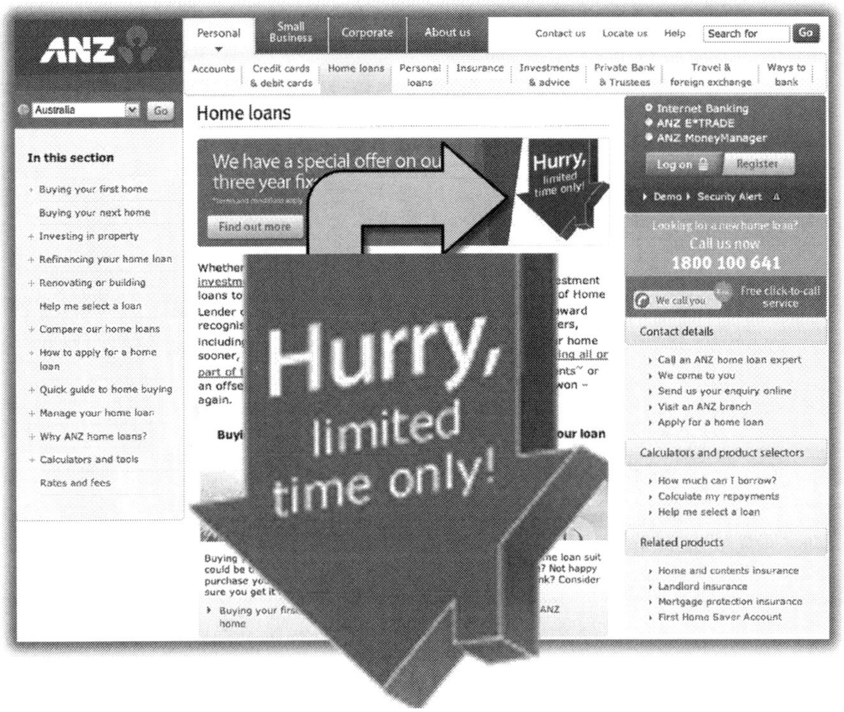

Whether you should lock yourself into a fixed rate requires careful consideration and is definitely not something that you should do in a rush. On the bright side, ANZ does make mention that a Fixed Rate loan isn't for everyone and that it can result in hefty penalties if you decide to bunk out early… Although that warning might be read by more people if it was at the top of the ad rather than sitting at the bottom of a separate, downloadable document outlining the terms and conditions.

Taking the right steps in identifying the most effective mortgage for your needs is crucial. If it turns out to be Resi, ANZ or any other merchant and they really want your business, they will waive those fees, give you those discounts or offer you that rate anyway. If they won't, they simply value your business less today than they did back then.

It's not just the risk of choosing the wrong lender that you need to worry about either. Rushing in can also result in:

- Choosing expensive, inappropriate loan features.
- Paying more on costly fees than you should.
- Missing out on valuable features that might reduce the interest you pay, the time it takes to repay your loan and the time involved in looking after your finances.
- Borrowing more than you should.
- Missing the catch and trapping yourself between staying with a lemon loan and paying a hefty penalty to hit the eject button.

Your mortgage is a big…hang on… a MASSIVE financial commitment that can improve, maintain or ruin your happiness. Take your time and get it right.

Paying retail

There's a bunch of different ways merchants trick us into thinking we are getting a great deal. As we've recently discussed, one of those methods is to offer you X% off their standard variable rate. Like retailers that mark prices up to mark them down at sale time, you might wind up making some kind of saving, however it's usually nowhere near as big as you might think because at the end of the day, you're still paying retail.

Even if you got the retail 'X% off standard variable' deal, what many borrowers don't realise because most merchants won't promote it, is that you can easily save a further $57,000 on the average mortgage. And I do mean easily.

Which raises the question of why on earth would you ever pay retail on your mortgage?

The likely answer is that you hadn't heard that you could save more money on your loan without extra payments and effort; or you just thought that it was not possible. But it is. The other important question for merchants is how they can claim to have your interests at heart, yet urge you to pay retail knowing you can get the exact same loan, same lender, same features and same repayments for $57,000 less? Contrary to what the MFAA tells us, merchants recommending you to pay retail put their commission ahead of your best interests. It is that simple.

> *"Look after the pennies and the dollars will look after themselves"*
> *J. Paul Getty December 15, 1892 – June 6, 1976*

The good news is, you could save even more once you finish absorbing Mortgage Free, Debt Free then apply all of your new found knowledge. But for now, let's quickly focus on how to avoid paying retail.

For most of this decade, brokers have been sharing lender paid commissions with the borrowers whose loans create them. Called cashback mortgage brokers, the part these guys will pay you ranges anywhere from a little to a lot. I should know. In 2003, I invented the method that, even today delivers you <u>the largest</u> cashback savings available - regular, ongoing rebates of your trail commission. Five years on and I sold my share of the business to become even more focussed on the interests of borrowers which of course, includes writing this book.

As you should now understand, the most lucrative commission by far is the trail commission. Trail is the bit that helps big franchised brokers to sell their franchises to everyday people. Once the broker has arranged the mortgage; the trail commission is passive income. i.e. you don't have to do a great deal except make sure the borrower is okay then sit back and receive a commission payment every month. What could be better than that?

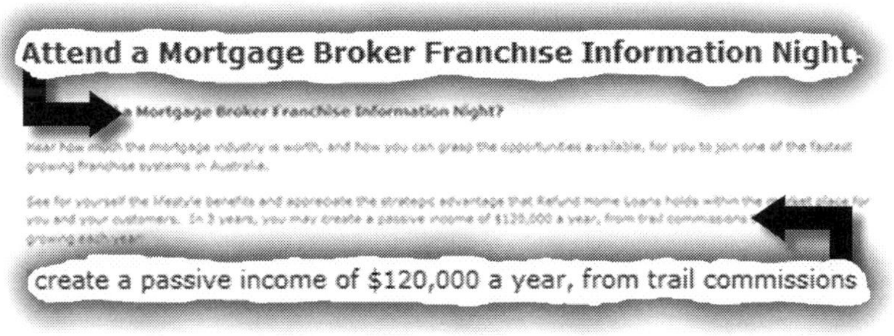

Trail commission is so significant that Mortgage Choice mentioned it repeatedly in their 2004 prospectus and in glowing terms to induce investors making statements such as "Trail commissions also generate higher margins". In layman's terms, this means more profit for less effort. So if it is important and profitable to the big end of town, it should be important to you too. After all, you're the one footing the bill.

Signing on the spot

In sales speak, there is a term known as the presumptive close. It's when the person doing the selling feels like they have covered all your objections and won you over, so they move in for the kill....er close.

In the mortgage world, your 'consultant' will reach into their briefcase or drawer or open a folder and pull out an application form. Cocky merchants will 'just start to fill it out' to 'save you time' once you have made your decision.

By all means let them go for it. But when they are done, fold it up and set it aside. Don't sign anything until they have given you a firm quote that you can objectively compare with any other option from any other source.

Falling for freebies

According to an old proverb, "The best things in life are free" and I couldn't agree more. However when they coined that notion, they were talking about things that actually are free. Love, friendship, honesty, hope. There is no way in a zillion years they were ever talking about choosing the right mortgage.

You can NEVER trust 'free professional' advice, so why waste life listening to it? There's another old expression that advice is worth what you pay for it. While good advice pays for itself, 'free professional advice' on such a significant financial decision as your mortgage often winds up being very costly.

> *"It's not what you pay them, it's how much they cost you"*
> *Neil Jenman*

It doesn't really matter whether your 'adviser' is a lender or a mortgage broker. Merchants are always selling, even the ones who don't realise it. Like when you hit the brakes if someone jumps out in front of your car, merchants sell because that's what they practice all day long. It's automatic. So whenever they are talking to you about your mortgage, you can never be certain whether a merchant is saying something important that you really need to know, or just talking about the things that help them 'get the sale'.

Asking a debt merchant for their opinion on any of the following is like asking "how much money would you like to make at my expense?"

- ✗ Which Loan is right for me?

- Which Lender has the best one of those?
- What Loan Term should I take?
- How much should I borrow?
- Should I take a Fixed or Variable Rate?
- Is Interest only right for me?
- How long should I take Interest Only for?
- How can I lower my repayments?

Aside from the mortgage and finance industry, I can't think of any 'professional' that promises free advice on anything they are professionally qualified to advise on. Can you?

By the way, you should also keep your eyes peeled for the worst of the worst, the Cake Pigs. These are the merchants who like to eat their cake and have it too. They'll charge you a fee AND collect nice, fat commissions for the entire time you remain in debt. Oink, oink.

Blind leaps of faith

Staying with the theme of barnyard analogies for just a moment, my father is fond of saying "If it walks like a duck, talks like a duck and has feathers, it's probably a duck". But there's that wriggle room again, 'probably'. Let's face it, if you've never really heard a duck talk (and I haven't), then it could be a goose, a chicken, or even a person in a duck suit.

Just because a person wears a business suit or uniform, speaks the jargon, has big brand backing, and maintains accreditation with an association or even makes an appearance in the press doesn't mean they are going to offer good information or advice. In fact the Mortgage Choice broker interviewed for "Getting more from your lender" which ran in a major Sydney newspaper, not only has all of that, he has dozens of testimonials to affirm his skill. He has also had the benefit of more than five years of Mortgage Choice training and experience to boot.

Although there's plenty in this article to raise the eyebrows, the standout winner by far is the quote from Mortgage Choice, "The interest-only route also achieves the biggest savings compared to a capital repayment mortgage…"

Ummm. Bollox.

As impressive and unfamiliar as the term 'capital repayment mortgage' may be, it's been lifted from the UK market, not ours. In Australia, we call them principal and interest loans or simply P&I.

Buying on an interest only basis never costs the same, it never costs you less and it always costs you more. When I say more, I'm not talking about a little more, I mean a LOT more.

Of course, you don't just pay more to the lender; the lender pays more commission to Mortgage Choice as well. You can be almost certain that some of this incentive filters down to the brokers in some way or another.

How much extra will it cost you on an average mortgage? You will be reaching into your pocket for an extra $241,942 on a 25-year loan - In fact, buying 'on an interest-only basis' for just the first year then switching to principal and interest still costs you about $6,000 extra!

Of course it's not just the lender that will make a lot more from you, the mortgage broker will too. "How much?" I hear you ask. Well, sticking with the average and taking a 25 year loan term, NAB would pay around twelve thousand dollars in extra commission for its Homeside range paid interest only versus the same loan paid principal and interest.

That's an extra 66% in commission from the bank to the broker just for helping you 'save' on monthly repayments. Pretty nice huh?

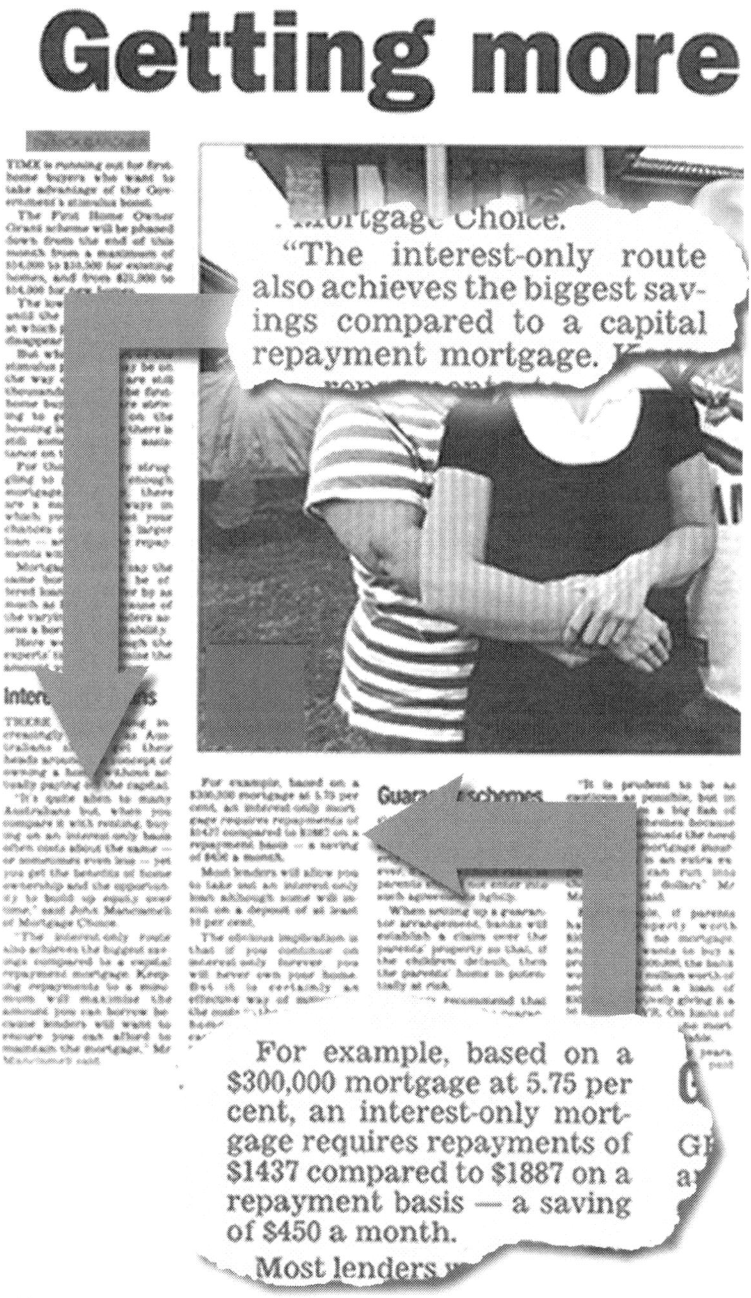

Getting more

...ortgage Choice.

"The interest-only route also achieves the biggest savings compared to a capital repayment mortgage. ...

For example, based on a $300,000 mortgage at 5.75 per cent, an interest-only mortgage requires repayments of $1437 compared to $1887 on a repayment basis — a saving of $450 a month.

Most lenders ...

Sorry Mortgage Choice, but you're wrong. Paying interest-only always costs borrowers more. Perhaps you're confused with the fact that interest-only usually earns you a LOT more commission.

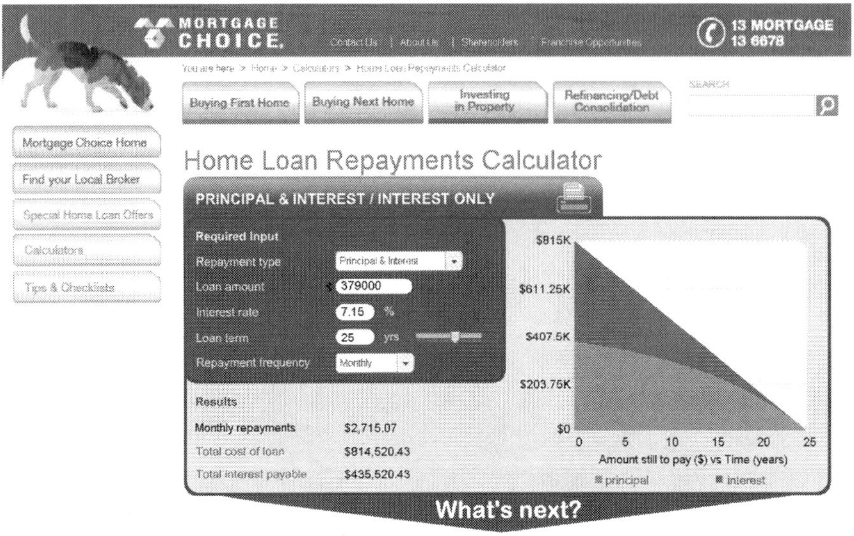

If Mortgage Choice took the time to check their theory that interest-only achieves the biggest savings compared to a capital repayment mortgage, they would realise their calculations agree with mine. Paying interest only <u>always</u> costs you more.

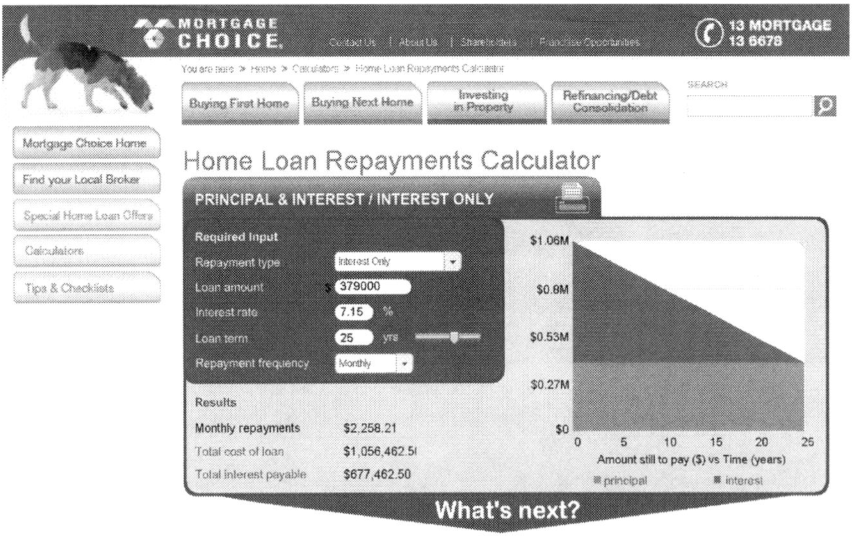

The Mortgage Choice calculator also demonstrates how props like a clever chart can distract you from crucial information. The dark shaded sections at the top of each chart are your interest costs. Compare the Principal and Interest chart at the top of the page from the interest-only chart at the bottom and you could be forgiven for not realising that paying interest only costs you about 60% more.

Loan Term	Buying Principal and Interest You Pay	Buying 1 Year Interest Only Extra Cost	Buying 5 Years Interest Only Extra Cost	Full Term Buying Interest Only Extra Cost
20 Years	$334,425	$7,649	$40,983	$207,545
25 Years	$435,520	$6,384	$34,397	$241,942
30 Years	$542,525	$5,259	$28,488	N-A

The above table demonstrates the extra interest you pay for 'buying on an interest-only basis' rather than paying Principal and Interest over the same loan term. Most lenders limit interest-only to 25 years.

Interest only has its place for some borrowers, which is why you can learn about it in detail later in this book. It has its own section because interest only also comes with serious risks and incredibly high costs if is misused or misunderstood. None of these were discussed in the article. It's all ra-rah, ra-rah, I can help you borrow more and 'save' you money along the way. Hmmm.

Regardless, buying property on an Interest only basis always costs more. Was Mortgage Choice misquoted; are they that bad at simple math; is their software defective; or is it about making more commission? To be fair, it could also be a tiny misunderstanding that could wind up costing you big time.

If it walks like a duck, talks like a duck and has feathers, it might be good for roasting. But whatever you do, don't listen to it.

Buying an out of date rate

It's pretty obvious that advertising can go out of date and the rate you are looking at in an old ad might not be the rate that applies today. That's not what I am calling an "out of date rate". I'm talking about the lender practice of "Holding back".

Holding back happens after a Reserve Bank rate rise and is where a lender deliberately delays announcing their own rate hikes until well after competitors have increased theirs.

When the Reserve Bank (the RBA) increases rates, it prompts a raft of consumers to think about whether there might be a better deal out there for them. These consumers often swell the market, creating opportunity for clever merchants to sell new loans by snatching customers away from competitors who lifted rates too soon. Then there's always the brand new borrowers that were already looking.

Lenders holding back rates cash in on the perception they offer a 'cheaper rate'. The lender knows that by the time your loan settles, or soon after, it jumps up to the real rate. Your lender also knows that, with or without exit penalties, those first few months are the time you are least likely to vote with your feet.

Whenever the Reserve Bank lifts rates it creates an undeniable pressure for lenders to lift their rates too. Although I am happy to be corrected, I cannot recall once in the last 20 years when the RBA increased rates and lenders have not increased their own rates by the RBA amount or more.

The truth is that when it comes to variable rate loans, lenders can increase rates at the drop of a hat. They don't have to tie their variable rate to the RBA in either the size of any rate change, or the timing of it. It's just strategically convenient and when lenders mostly move in a pack, consumers are left with little choice but to be trampled.

Although holding back is unfair and dangerous to consumers, it is currently legal. Due to increased competition and the general success of this trick, lenders have started to exploit this type of promotion more regularly. There is no prescribed legal obligation for merchants to advertise when they last changed their interest rate or by how much, even though there should be.

Listening to Johnny

When I was a little kid, I did a lot of stupid stuff, mostly because my friends did it too. I can't exactly remember who lead who into doing what, but it doesn't really matter. My mum would often say, "If Johnny jumped off the bridge, would you jump too?"

Toward the end of my teenage years, mum's words echoed in my memory. I watched in disbelief as my mate Johnny actually did jump off a bridge. Swimming back to the shore all smiling and proud, Johnny urged his friends, including me to do it too. Some did. I didn't. What none of us realised, including Johnny, is that he had actually caused himself a very serious injury that only surfaced years later. It completely changed his life, robbing him of years of freedom and happiness that he really should have been able to experience.

Unlike Johnny's broken neck, mortgage mistakes often harm people's financial health so gradually, they may never even realise the severity or cost of the damage they have done.

At the start of Mortgage Free, Debt Free, you read some extracts from the positions vacant advertisements posted by banks, building societies, credit unions, lenders and brokers. Debt merchants. Besides sales ability one of the consistent, sought after skills is networking, more commonly known as building a referral source. It's where merchants get to you through your network of trusted and respected people. Your dad, your mum, your sister, brother or mate who just got their 'loan sorted'.

They are all nice people and no doubt with good intentions; however they are likely to have made at least two of the common costly mistakes you are learning to avoid now. Don't let their good intentions cost you. Do them a favour and buy them a copy of Mortgage Free, Debt Free. Make them pay you for it too. Otherwise it's free advice, and we all know how dangerous that can be. Remember "if Johnny jumped off the bridge, would you jump too?"

Think independently. Do your own research. Hire professionals if you need to. Ignore Johnny.

Falling for the headline

Although there is no formal definition of 'headline rate', common sense ought to tell you that it's the interest rate the merchants like to put in the spotlight. This can be entirely different to the effective rate that you wind up paying and completely disconnected from how much the loan costs you in interest, fees and charges (this is called Total Individual Cost and we'll talk a little more on that soon).

Of all of the different mortgage products available, there is one type you should approach with extreme caution, or better still avoid altogether. The introductory rate mortgage. There are quite a few different versions of these types of loans; however the basic premise of the trickier ones is the same:

1. It has an initial period with an attractive rate (which is often rolled out as the headline rate).

2. The merchant offers advertising comparisons to competitors' loans with superior functionality.

3. There is one or more scheduled rate hikes over the first few years (which are on top of any Reserve Bank or competition induced rate rises).

4. Advertising, marketing and merchant information emphasises the headline rate or minimum repayment even though it is short lived.

5. The lender traps you at a higher, often uncompetitive rate for several years using ugly penalties not reflected in Advertised Comparison Rates.

As an example at the time I researched Mortgage Free, Debt Free, a popular, award winning home loan, which I will call 'The

Intro' had an introductory rate of 5.70% for a couple of years before stepping up to a rate of 6.00%. Whether these rates seem good or bad to you at the time you are reading this doesn't really matter, it's the principles that you need to focus on. The rates on this loan will move up and down and the rest of the market will move along as well.

As you would expect, the lender selling The Intro works very hard to sharpen your focus on the headline rate of 5.70%. It's always the first rate they mention and they also have clever campaigns with simple supplementary messages like "1% below the banks standard variable".

Right now, the 5.70% rate is quite competitive; however you can beat it. Even paying retail it's also very easy to beat the rate The Intro jumps up to, which is 6.00%. Of course, the merchant keeps reminding you how much cheaper their rates are compared to the bank 'Standard Variable Rate'. Hmmm.

However, at the same time, there is a prominent bank that offers a very similar loan in terms of the functions of The Intro. I'll call this loan The Bank. The Bank has a rate of 5.94%. It is not an introductory rate loan, so there is no step up rate.

Taking the average loan amount of $379,000, which mortgage do you think works out cheaper and by how much?

Quick Tip:

Ugly penalty fees have a range of different names (Deferred Establishment Fee, Early Payout Fee, Break Cost and more). They do not have to be advertised anywhere.

Although you may have your own personal view of what an Ugly fee is, I work on the basis that $500 is a bit rough, $1000 is pretty unattractive and anything more is definitely UGLY.

Get a written quote prior to making an application to see these fees before it's too late. You'll read about the simple and most reliable way to do this very soon.

If you focussed on the headline rate like the merchant selling The Intro wants you to, you would probably expect The Bank would be more expensive, but have no idea by how much.

Take a more holistic, educated guess and you probably think both merchants' costs are similar, but have no idea how close. If you properly calculate a Total Individual Cost (assuming no LMI), you will discover The Bank comes out ahead by around $1,000. Whoppededoo you might be tempted to think.

However, by taking The Bank, and using The Free Money Strategy, The Bank becomes $28,000 cheaper on current interest rates. However to quote Tim Shaw, "but wait, there's more".

Right now interest rates are at the super cheap end of the 'normal range' so it's reasonable to expect rates to increase. In fact it's unreasonable not to expect rates to rise at different times throughout the life of any mortgage. As this happens, The Intro falls even further behind The Bank. Adding just 1.2% to each interest rate takes both products closer to the average variable interest rate over the last 15 years. When you do this, the gap widens to over $35,000. Increase your loan term to 30 years and you are now talking about paying over $55,000 extra for The Intro.

	The Intro	The Bank + Free Money	Saving
Current Rates			
25 Years	$351,060	$322,620	$28,439
Normalised Rates			
25 Years	$436,612	$401,165	$35,447
30 Years	$544,533	$488,883	$55,650

The table above shows the difference in Total Individual Cost between The Intro and The Bank using The Free Money Strategy.

Although not true for all introductory rate loans The Free Money Strategy could not be used with The Intro at the time of writing. Of course, THEY won't tell you that, but I will.

By the way, introductory rates are often just the lure to get you through the door. Once you're inside, you often find yourself talking about a completely different 'better value' mortgage.

Fall for the headline and you will pay a very high price, so just don't do it.

The Free Money Strategy...

An interest saver strategy which legally uses other people's money to repay your mortgage.

The higher the interest rates go, the more money you will save with the Free Money Strategy and we'll learn how you can use it shortly.

Target fixation

There is a stretch of the Old Pacific Highway just north of Sydney which, on sunny weekends long since past, echoed the roar of motorcyclists washing off the stress of the modern working week. Tight twisting corners, short fast straights and the odd open bend, 'the old road' carves its way through some of Sydney's most beautiful bushland and spectacular Hawkesbury sandstone. It was once a favourite with bike riders however much of the unofficial racing that was once common, has disappeared since society started to become more responsible. Police were huge fans too. It was easy to top up their quotas at the expense of overzealous weekend warriors who thought the posted speed limit was a vague guide for newbies rather than an actual limit. (Just kidding Officers, I know there's no such thing as a ticket quota...)

Along the way was a rather shabby shack perched somewhat randomly on the side of the old road, seemingly in the middle of nowhere. "Pie in the Sky" did a roaring trade every weekend when the sun was shining as a favoured spot for reenergised riders to kick back, have a bite to eat and exchange war stories.

Although the old road was in fair condition, some of the bends were cut sharply into the hill. At certain times of the year these bends barely, if ever, saw sunlight. Moss grew in these parts which, with the almost always damp road, made these sections very slippery. If you picked the wrong line, they were downright deadly. Of course like any Sydney road there were also the mandatory potholes generously scattered along the way, often at the most inconvenient of places. However for experienced riders, that all just added to the fun and excitement.

Sitting at the Pie in the Sky you would regularly hear stories of newbies disappearing into the bushland at speed after loosing control from a pothole or slippery patch that they ought to have seen and been able to avoid. Whenever it happened, the outcome for the rider was never good.

As news of an accident reached the riders at the Pie, it would ripple randomly through the individual groups and the entire atmosphere would go just a little quiet, almost awkward. Riders looked at each other with a mixture of disbelief and a kind of sadness, even though most didn't know the victim. A momentary silence, then someone would knowingly murmur "target fixation". Some time later, "Target fixation" came the softly spoken answer.

Target fixation is when you become so focussed on something that you stop thinking about, looking for, or reacting to other things that may actually be more important to your outcome. Merchants love it because a target fixated borrower is easy to misdirect, like a blinkered horse is easier to lead.

Common costly targets which capture the focus of many borrowers at their own peril include:

- Lowest Rate.
- No Ongoing Fees.
- No Fees.
- Need approval before ….
- No Application Fees.
- No bells and whistles.
- No valuation Fee.
- Big four bank.
- Star Ratings or Award winners.
- Wanting the same bank as your father, mother, brother, sister, partner, friend.

Missing the catch

That's catch as in snag, trip or trap. While there's a bunch of them out there, one of the more devious, not so little catches introduced by lenders is the Deferred Establishment Fee. Well at least that's what some lenders call it. Others might label it a 'DEF', 'Break Cost', 'Early Payout Penalty' and 'Early Discharge Fee'.

Mention Deferred Establishment Fees to a merchant and most will race to defend them, explaining this family of nasty fees keeps the entry and ongoing costs of your loan down. Bull.

Merchants simply want to make it easy and attractive for you to buy from them and harder for you to leave before they have extracted their pound of flesh. Not surprisingly, these hefty, 'unascertainable' fees don't show up in Advertised Comparison Rates. If you still think you can rely on Comparison Rates, then not only am I rubbish at what I do, but you probably won't realise just how badly the deck has been stacked against you until it's too late.

When you see a Deferred Establishment Fee, you should think of it as the bet you place that:

- Your lender won't increase rates willy nilly and independent of what the other lenders or the Reserve Bank of Australia does.
- You've seen, understand and accept all the fees your lender will charge you.
- Your lender won't add new or increase existing fees.
- Your lender continues to deliver on service.
- You know it, you've done it and you haven't missed anything important in making your loan selection.

Had you placed that bet in the last five years, you would have certainly lost. To make sure you have the mobility which keeps your loan competitive:

- ✓ Be wary of any loan with a penalty of up to $1,000.
- ✓ Be EXTREMELY wary of penalties above $1,000.
- ✓ Calculate the dollar cost of the penalty if your lender uses clever words such as 1.2% of your original loan amount; one month's repayment or formula type penalty.
- ✓ Don't let the spin bamboozle you. Lenders know Deferred Establishment Fees are a win-win for them and a lose-lose for you.

Not to be outdone, at least one merchant is double dipping on its Deferred Establishment Fee by splitting early payout penalties under a Deferred Establishment Fee and the Discharge Fee.

Deferred Establishment Fee you only need to pay DEF if you pay out the loan with in the first five years.	$1,500 (Year 1 & 2) $1,000 (Year 3 & 4) $500 (Year 5)
Discharge Fee	$715 for (Year 1-5) $215 thereafter

The marketing team must have thought it would look bad to have a Deferred Establishment Fee starting as high as $2,000 and remaining as high as $1,000 even in the fifth year. Instead they buried $500 under the Discharge Fee for the first five years. I bet the clever chappy who thought that up can afford a new set of wheels for his Ferrari.

A traditional Discharge Fee is a fixed fee purely to cover the legal costs of discharging the mortgage once the loan has ended. It should be no more than a couple of hundred dollars. Using a Discharge Fee as some kind of penalty is downright horrible.

Of course it's not the fee that's the issue. The problem is how it is hidden from your view; brushed aside by merchants as unimportant or dressed up in clever spin.

An example of merchant spin on fees

I encountered one of the most entertaining examples of spin I have ever read whilst skimming a Facts and Fees brochure of a highly awarded lender. Buried on the last page under the heading of OTHER FACTS was a sentence which read:

"With one of the lowest rate, fully featured variable rate home loans in Australia... why would you ever want to leave!"

Why indeed? If you're struggling to think of five likely and massive reasons, flip back to the previous page and look for the "**x**".

However for this particular lender, you don't even have to 'leave' to cop a knifing. The Deferred Establishment Fee can be triggered simply by reducing your credit limit or making too many extra payments. Granted the threshold is 50%, but the point is, they will punish you even if you stay with them. The penalty for our average loan? $5,695 in the first couple of years. Ouch.

It's hard to know exactly how this multi award winning merchant continues to sell loans, but here's a clue. They win awards; their Advertised Comparison Rate is moderately competitive; they're not a bank and they can scream NO ONGOING FEES.

They also have an Application Fee of just 0.66% with only two other set-up fees that amount to a few hundred dollars. To a careless borrower, the cost of setting up the loan probably seems quite small. It isn't. On our average $379,000 mortgage, that means an upfront cost of almost $3,350 and that's assuming you're not paying any mortgage insurance. That's actually enormous.

However once they rope you in, they can hike the rate, drop their service (which beyond sales may never have been there in the first place) and sting you with massive fees when you want to make changes. The total cost to vote with your feet in the first three years?

$9,041.

Don't miss catches. They won't miss you.

Getting trapped in the web

Because there are so many lenders and loan options to choose from, most borrowers will quickly cull a list of over a thousand different options down to just a handful and in some cases, just one or two. This is called making a shortlist and many borrowers start out by creating a short list of the 'better value' options using the Internet. Worse still, some people actually apply for loans based on little more than an internet ad.

No doubt the internet is an amazing place full of all sorts of information. Good and bad. It vaguely falls under free advice, but then most people don't think of the stuff they find on the web as advice. It's more like free information, and that dear reader is where the problem begins. For some reason, otherwise intelligent people can place too much confidence on the information they discover on the web.

A major challenge of choosing your loan using the internet is that the pool of lenders and products you start out with will always be incomplete and inaccurate. Not sometimes, always. Worse still, while you might work out how inaccurate the information is, you will never know just how incomplete it is.

GIGO tells us that if your short list is selected from unreliable information, you wind up with a shorter, but still unreliable, list of options. If your short list is rubbish, then the best outcome you could ever hope for is a mortgage which is the best of a bad lot. The cream of the crap.

In case you didn't know it, the internet is more like one big advertisers market than it is a library or reference centre. Sure, some sites are built to provide specific, useful services, however most are purely there as an advertising platform. Mistaking advertising for reliable, independent information that you can base decisions on is very silly, yet a surprising number of people do just that.

Take the web site www.ratecity.com.au. Thanks to a remarkably successful advertising campaign and the heavy support of major shareholder Canstar CANNEX, Rate City has the hallmarks of a website you should be able to trust as a source of reliable mortgage help and information. It looks like a self serve interest rate reference site packed with useful, independent and reliable information. As far as these types of sites go, it is without doubt one of the better ones out there, which might sound promising, but doesn't actually say that much. Like all the 'free information' websites and perhaps some you pay for, Rate City is one whopping, fat advertisement. An infomercial, advertorial or whatever other fancy name the marketers can create.

For the moment at least, these websites escape any real responsibility to you for the mortgage information that they provide. In the case of Rate City, that information can be out of date (i.e. wrong) and often have gaps with no real impact to them, however the impact to you if you rely on that information could be massive and long lasting.

Like most of these types of websites, Rate City does not list any lender that won't pay them a fee and they don't always tell you the most important things you need to know about that lender or their loans. So Rate City is more like a lazy, apathetic mortgage broker than a reliable, independent, mortgage reference site. They're paid by the lenders to promote loans to you, even though they really know nothing about you, your plans, or your situation. In fact they have virtually no legal obligation to provide you with any reliable help when it comes to choosing your mortgage.

And like mortgage brokers, Rate City doesn't offer all loans for the lenders that pay them kick backs either. At least that's how it appears. Unlike a broker, it's actually hard to determine the full list of lenders Rate City is tied into.

As a quick test, I searched for Owner Occupied, 3 Year Fixed Rates for all States using Rate City's search function.

This search returned just 33 results. Instinct and experience tells me that this is a low number as it is less than most independent mortgage brokers would be able to arrange, which, up to now, had been my low tide mark.

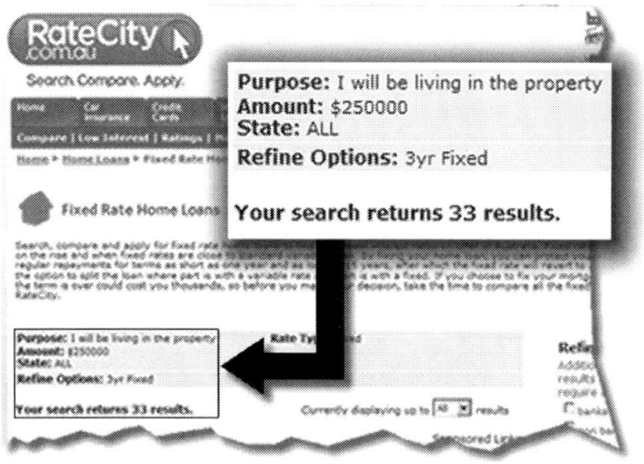

This is a sample search of all 3 Year Fixed Rates on Rate City.

This very selective list is also a lot less than the 114 results their part owner and information provider Canstar CANNEX reports in its Home Loan Star Ratings Report.

Looking a little closer at the results I notice quite a few different things that should worry you. Perhaps the most obvious is the two rates advertised for nab, 7.59% and 7.69%.

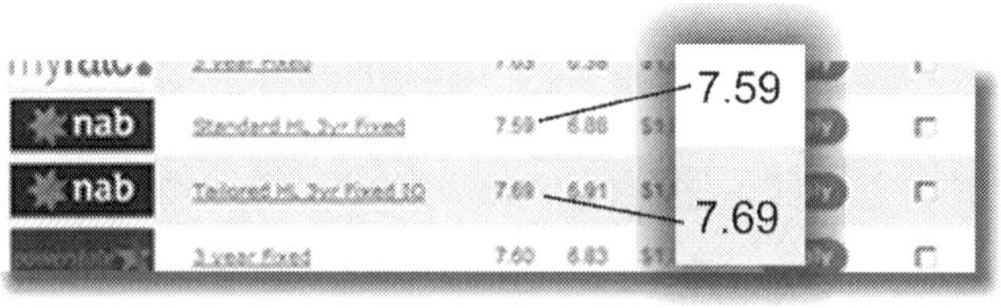

The only NAB loans advertised from the search when the list is sorted alphabetically by lender.

The good news is these rates are correct. Well at least the ones that are there are correct anyway. The bad news is:

- NAB offers SIX different rates for this product type, not just the TWO that Rate City advertised.
- These rates START at 7.39% which is a LOT less than the lowest advertised product at 7.59%.
- THREE of FOUR rates available through NAB and NOT mentioned have rates LOWER than the ones Rate City has advertised.

			NAB Choice Package and NAB Portfolio Facility[4]	
	Interest Rate	Comparison Rate	Interest Rate	Comparison Rate
FIXED RATE HOME LOANS (NAB Tailored Home Loan)				
1 year	6.59% pa	6.63% pa	6.49% pa	6.32% pa
2 years	7.29% pa	6.78% pa	7.19% pa	6.52% pa
3 years	LISTED 7.59% pa	6.9[illegible]	MISSING 7.49% pa	6.72% pa
4 years	7.69% pa	7.07% pa	7.59% pa	6.89% pa
5 years	7.89% pa	7.25% pa	7.79% pa	7.11% pa
10 years	8.09% pa	7.81% pa	7.99% pa	7.81% pa
Interest Only in Advance				
1 year	6.49% pa		6.39% pa	
2 years	7.19% pa		7.09% pa	
3 years	MISSING 7.49% pa		MISSING 7.39% pa	
4 years	7.59% pa		7.49% pa	
5 years	7.79% pa		7.69% pa	
Interest Only in Arrears				
1 year	6.69% pa	6.63% pa	6.59% pa	6.30% pa
2 years	7.39% pa	6.78% pa	7.29% pa	6.49% pa
3 years	LISTED 7.69% pa	6.9[illegible]	MISSING 7.59% pa	6.70% pa
4 years	7.79% pa	7.08% pa	7.69% pa	6.88% pa
5 years	7.99% pa	7.28% pa	7.89% pa	7.11% pa

nab

Interest Rates for Home Lending

Monday, 11 January 2010

The loans indicated as LISTED are (a) the options with the higher rate and (b) the only ones that were advertised in the search of www.ratecity.com.au.

So if you are thinking of visiting Rate City or any similar website make sure you:

1. Understand that it's a 'some care taken, no responsibility accepted' environment.

2. Click a few APPLY buttons if you want the rich to get richer because that's how these websites make money.

3. Remember GIGO.

While it might be fine to use these types of websites as a starting point, they fall well short of what it takes to get your loan right. If you think options you have found at Rate City sound good, by all means include them on your shopping list however get a proper credit quote before making an application.

Soon we will learn how to correctly structure your loan, obtain "you-friendly", not "merchant-friendly" credit quotes, access the most competitive deals in the market place and make reliable comparisons for yourself.

In the meantime, try not to get trapped in the web.

From time to time you may read website recommendations in Mortgage Free Debt Free such as www.proconsumer.com.au, www.borrowersagent.org and www.keyfacts.com.au.

Although these websites provide valuable templates, tools and information, they do not provide spot quotes on interest rates or product features. These sites are provided free of charge to consumers, lenders, agents and merchants and it is difficult and costly to deliver enough reliable, understandable information for you to make a loan short list, let alone actual loan selection.

Any website offering interest rate or loan comparisons and claiming to be complete, current, reliable and FREE is having you on.

Remember, a small omission by a website might cost them nothing but cost you dearly. And in this world, it's buyer beware.

Fast Facts

- ✓ Canstar CANNEX, is a financial research company best known for its Star Ratings.
- ✓ Lenders pay CANNEX thousands each year to get a Star Rating (the last time I checked it was at least $13,000).
- ✓ Canstar CANNEX also owns a major share of the mortgage and credit advertising website www.ratecity.com.au.
- ✓ Although it did for many years, CANNEX no longer calls itself 'independent' however merchants still do.
- ✓ Lenders must purchase services including Star Ratings from CANNEX to be listed on www.ratecity.com.au.
- ✓ Lenders pay Rate City around $75 each time a consumer clicks through to the lender.
- ✓ Information including interest rates and charges promoted by Canstar CANNEX can be incomplete and/or incorrect.
- ✓ CANNEX Star Ratings offer more expensive lenders the ability to still appear at the top of popular product lists.

Borrower: I want a mortgage with no fees.

Merchant: You want a mortgage with no fees? No problem, we've got those.

Borrower: I don't want to pay a high rate either.

Merchant: Sure, we've got one of the lowest rates around.

Two Weeks Later

Smart Borrower: Hey, I got my loan contracts today.

Merchant: Great, have you signed them?

Smart Borrower: Not yet. I read them first. There's a fee in here for solicitor's settlement charges. You said there were no fees.

Merchant: Oh that? That's not a fee, it's a disbursement. Everyone charges them.

Smart Borrower: What about the $8,960 I have to pay for Lenders Mortgage Insurance?

Merchant: That? Everyone will charge you LMI. There are only two insurers around, so it'll cost pretty much the same wherever you go.

Smart Borrower: Really? My agent called another lender who has given us a written quote of $5,500 and it's with the same insurer too. The settlement charges are a fixed fee of $150 and their interest rate turns out to be less than the advertised rates and less than yours. Will you match it to keep my business?

Merchant: Probably not, but there's gotta be a catch you haven't spotted yet. Make sure they can settle your loan on time and aren't just making empty promises to win you over. Give me a call if I can help out any other way. My mobile's on 24/7.

Smart Borrower: Nice try. Goodbye.

Being busy or feeling stupid

In life learning is infinite. All of us suffer from ignorance which is why I have a core rule. Don't understand it? Don't do it. Life can seem too busy and getting the right mortgage too complicated. It is tempting and unfortunately common for borrowers to throw caution to the wind, signing on the dotted line, even though we don't understand potentially expensive detail.

While this might be an 'okay' idea if you have retained a borrowers agent to protect you, it is very dangerous if you are dealing with a merchant by using a broker or going the do-it-yourself route directly with the lender.

'If you don't understand the GST, don't vote for it.'
Paul Keating days out from the 1993 Election

Quite simply, if you don't understand why you are taking a certain loan, loan term, or feature, then you must ask the basic, what, where, when, how and my personal favourite, why? If you are being promised savings, make sure they really are savings, not just lower repayments or the short lived lower rates that honeymoon and introductory loans provide. Ask for amortisation schedules which actually show how the savings eventuate over the full term of the loan or a reliable credit quote that shows those savings in shorthand.

Don't fall for the old 'monthly savings' or 'annual savings' line. Never assume that either a monthly or an annual saving is ongoing. A monthly saving may only occur in one month. An annual saving may only occur for the first year. When that month or year is over, you might be in for a very rude shock and find yourself losing money, not saving it.

Even if you have retained a borrower's agent, you should still make sure you understand and agree with the decisions they help you make.

If you find yourself feeling dumb, stupid or foolish and this is holding you back from asking questions, sack your agent and find another - same too if you choose to deal directly with a merchant, although you can't exactly sack them because they don't work for you in the first place.

Never do something that you don't understand because it may come with a set of problems and costs that you weren't aware that you were signing up for as well.

Mixing business with pleasure

With around 13,000 mortgage brokers and many more bank, building society and credit union staff making money in the home loan industry, you are bound to either know one of them or have a friend or family member who knows one of them, especially if they are good 'networkers'.

Although it is reasonably common for borrowers looking for help to turn to the people within their family or friendship circle who are 'in the business', it is a very big mistake from a borrowers perspective. Mortgages aren't Tupperware and making a bad choice or getting bad advice is a completely different kettle of fish to choosing a container that isn't microwavable. Besides exposing deeply personal information about your financial position, the risk of fallout to your financial health and your family can be horrendous. The stakes are higher because important personal relationships could also be lost or damaged.

Friends, family and their extended circle often benefit from an automatic trust and respect that they have not earned from you as a professional. If you met them for the very first time as a lender, mortgage broker or a borrowers agent it is likely you would scrutinise their credentials, advice and fees a lot more closely. You should do this even if they are family. There have been many falling outs between friends and family over money. If you really feel compelled to mix business with pleasure, rather than cutting them slack, you should raise your expectations because they should look after you a lot better than they would a complete stranger.

If your friend or family member is a mortgage broker, they will understand that commissions and bonuses deposited to your loan will help you get mortgage free faster by saving you buckets of interest as well as time. If they really care about you and the friendship you share then it's a no brainer that they will help you with this too.

If they play the disappointment card claiming they now feel you don't trust or respect them, strike an advice fee that represents a fair professional service charge that you are willing to pay. They should then have no qualms arranging your loan and rebating 100% of all commissions that the lender pays. That's upfront commission and trail commission. It's called a Pro Consumer Agreement because your mortgage broker is able to work for you, without commission pressure, whether they are a friend, family member or complete stranger. Although it's much better for you than getting help from an ordinary mortgage broker, it's still far less comprehensive than hiring a borrowers agent.

You will learn more about different types of professional help shortly. In the meantime it pays to remember that you can get 100% of the trail commissions from a complete stranger and you won't have to pay any fee at all. Friends should be able to do better than that.

Grabbing the tiger by the tail

As Julie Andrews sang, "start at the very beginning, a very good place to start". While the untrained often begin by talking about features, or rates or fees or even by purchasing a property before profiling their loan, there is only one proven way to get it right every time.

So let's get on with it.

"If you don't act now while it's fresh in your mind, it will probably join the list of things you were always going to do but never quite got around to.

Chances are you'll also miss some opportunities."
Paul Clitheroe

Revision: Avoid common costly mistakes

Look at you! You're charging ahead and already have a very solid understanding of how the local mortgage market place really works.

You have also learned about the most common mistakes made by borrowers every day of the week. In this section you hopefully built some rules for yourself like:

- ✓ Be mature and open minded.
- ✓ Don't rush in.
- ✓ Never Pay Retail.
- ✓ Reject free advice. It can be very costly.
- ✓ Never sign on the spot.
- ✓ Consider the whole picture.
- ✓ If you don't understand it, don't do it.
- ✓ Don't waste time comparing standard variable with any other loan or vice versa.
- ✓ Beware the web. Spiders aren't the only ones that use them to catch their prey.
- ✓ Forget the headline; it's the fine print that's important.
- ✓ It's best not to mix business with pleasure.

STEP 2

Choose your weapons

"Debt is the slavery of the free"
Publilius Syrus 1st Century AD

This crucial step is often thought about way too late or it is overlooked altogether. Borrowers, who take on a mortgage at the age of thirty, will hopefully live another sixty years or so. If you're happy to spend the first, healthiest and happiest half of that time with a sodding great debt, then you can skip this step.

For the rest of us, credit, while convenient and at times useful, is the enemy. Interest reduction strategies are the weapons you need to bring your enemy to its knees as quickly as possible.

There are five strategies that are either well known or have a real impact on the time and money it takes you to get debt free.

The "+10", "Savings Plan" and "The Free Money Strategy" are the easiest to use, require the least amount of discipline and deliver some of the best interest savings. Interestingly, these three aren't commonly promoted by the merchants.

Why do you think that is?

The 'Fortnight Payment Plan'

Okay, confession time. I'm not the world's greatest fan of the Fortnight Payment Plan as it requires too much time to make it work properly and just has too much 'magic'. Nonetheless, I have included the idea just in case you feel it's the right one for you - in which case you might as well do it properly. Without doubt, this is one of the most publicised and often misunderstood strategies.

If you implement the Fortnight Payment Plan properly you will definitely make solid interest savings. But then these savings are outdone by +10, which is far easier to manage and more reliable.

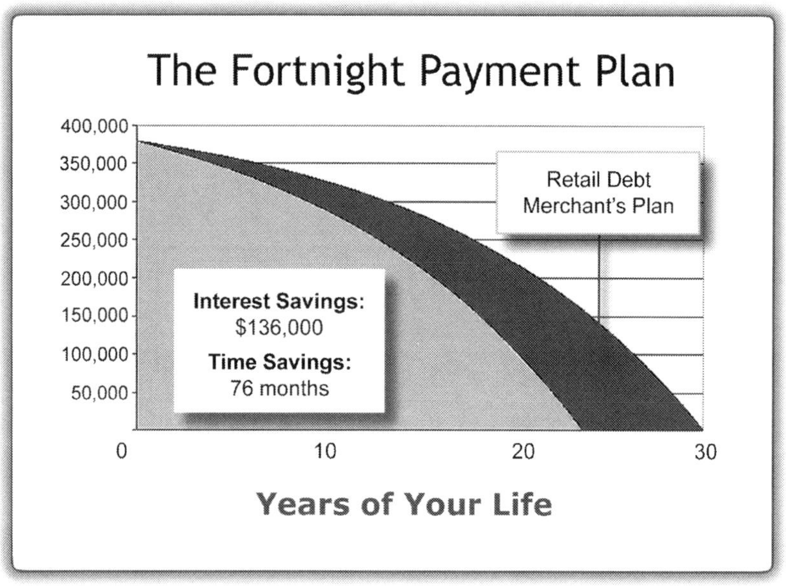

How it works

The Fortnight Payment Plan works by dividing your minimum monthly repayment by two, then paying that amount each fortnight. Like magic, this reduces the time to smash the average 25 year mortgage by a little more than 6 years.

Although many borrowers (and sadly, some merchants) think the interest saving comes from making payments more often, you are also making extra payments. It's these extra payments that really put the dent in your debt. For example, assume your minimum monthly repayment is $1,000. So:

Monthly Repayment = $1,000

Over a year you would repay:

12 x $1,000 = $12,000 each year

Instead, pay half the monthly repayment each fortnight:

$1,000 / 2 = $500 per fortnight

Over a year using this strategy, you would repay:

26 x $500 = $13,000 each year

Which is an extra annual payment of:

$13,000 - $12,000 = $1,000

And:

$1,000 = 1 x Magical Monthly Repayment

The 'magical' extra payment comes from a common perception that there are two fortnights to a month. Stop and think about that for a moment and you realise there are only 28 days in two fortnights, whereas most months have 31, February has either 28 or 29 days and the rest have 30. This means that every two fortnights, you are making 2 or 3 days of extra payments. Over the year, these add up to one extra monthly payment every year and that's the real reason it works.

To make it work you must

Look for a loan that ideally accepts fortnightly repayments and you must split the minimum monthly repayment in two and pay it each fortnight.

Each time there is a rate rise, you need to work out your monthly repayment. This means calling your lender, time on hold because the call centres get busiest after a rate rise, then when you finally talk to a person, you need to get out the calculator and divide it by two. Then of course, you have to change everything.

Ease of Use

It's a pain because it is so fiddly and means juggling your pay cycle with your mortgage repayment cycle to get it right.

Although fortnightly repayments are fairly commonplace, if your lender only does monthly, then you can wind up falling out of synch with repayment schedules.

The clunky nature of the Fortnight Payment Plan may be okay for a while, but a lot of people end up abandoning it. Worse still, a fair swag of the population misunderstand it, don't do it right and wind up thinking they are getting a benefit when they actually aren't.

Special Mortgage Functions

- Your mortgage must accept extra payments (preferably unlimited).

- This strategy works out a little easier to manage if your mortgage offers Fortnightly Repayments.

Watch out for

When you tell a lender you want to repay fortnightly, many will change the repayments to a fortnightly repayment (i.e. in the example, $12,000 each year / 26 payments). Whilst better than nothing, it does bugger all to reduce real interest costs.

Take a look at +10 which is the one they DON'T tell you about. It's easy to understand, implement, maintain and it works.

The +10

The +10, sometimes also called the GST strategy is one of the simplest and most reliable methods of reducing your interest costs and shortening the time it takes to repay your mortgage.

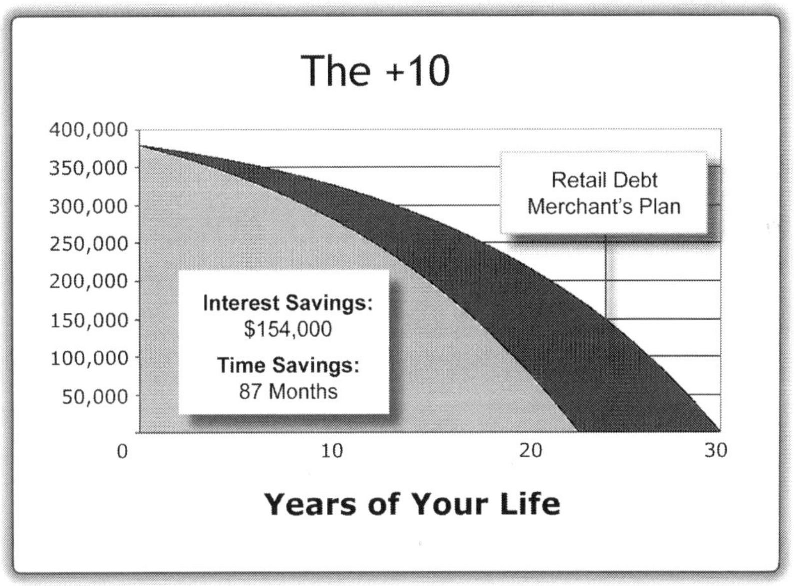

How it works

The +10 requires you to make small, extra payments each time you make your regular minimum repayment, however as you can see the results are definitely worth it. The +10 outstrips the Fortnight Payment Plan in savings, reducing interest costs on the average mortgage by over $154,000. It gets you mortgage free 7 and a bit years faster than simply paying the minimum lender repayments.

To make it work you must

+10 is simple, foolproof, within your reach and your control. All you need to do is set your regular weekly, fortnightly or monthly repayments 10% higher than the minimum repayment required by your lender.

Each time your lender changes the interest rate of your mortgage, they must notify you of your new minimum repayment. Simply get out your calculator and multiply that amount by 1.1, then set your repayment to the result by telling your payroll office or reprogramming your internet banking.

Ease of use

This one's easy. It works no matter how often you get paid and regardless of whether you have set your repayments for weekly, fortnightly or monthly.

And no phone queues, bank queues or any of that life sapping rubbish. See? I told you it was good.

Special Mortgage Features

- Your mortgage must accept extra payments (preferably unlimited).

Watch out for

There's nothing much to be wary of when setting this up as it is so versatile and simple. However you should watch out for lenders reducing your payments when interest rates fall. The best way to avoid this is not let your lender manage your repayments, but to do it yourself.

Quick Tip:

If possible, have your payroll office split your pay so that part of it is credited directly to your mortgage. This keeps you in control of just how quickly you get debt free.

If you can't do that, schedule your repayments yourself via internet banking to keep control and avoid the queues.

Want to put the +10 on turbo? Instead of topping up payments with 10% of your loan repayment, try 10% of your pay packet.

Okay, let's take a break from strategy and look at why you are WAY better off sticking extra money into your mortgage or a 100% Offset Account …

You don’t pay interest on money you don’t owe

Okay, this is not a strategy, but I thought you should learn why using your mortgage as your savings and goals account is smart. Keeping things simple, let’s call this money ‘savings’.

By banking savings into your mortgage, your debt is temporarily reduced by the value of your savings. This is called a principal reduction. You don’t owe that money so you don’t get charged interest on it which produces two financial benefits for most borrowers:

1. You’re ahead by the spread

Lenders charge you a higher rate of interest on your loans than they offer you on your deposits in a normal banking account. The difference between the rate paid for deposits and the rate charged for loans is known as the spread.

For example, a bank’s online deposit account might pay 3.50% p.a., however they charge 4.89% p.a. for mortgage loans.

Savings kept against your mortgage ‘earns’ you 4.89% p.a. because you don’t pay interest on that money. If you kept your savings in the online deposit account, you would be paid 3.50% which means you’re ahead by the spread:

$$4.89\% - 3.50\% = 1.39\% \text{ p.a.}$$

Instead of being paid 3.50%, you avoid shelling out 4.89% on that money!

2. Nett of tax advantage

When a bank pays you interest, the taxman calls it income, so you pay tax on it. However if you reduce the interest you pay on your loans, there's no tax to be paid as you are reducing expenses rather than earning an income. This produces a better after tax outcome[1].

So what does that exactly mean? Let's say you have saved $30,000 and assuming you are taxed at 33 cents in the dollar your options look like this:

Option 1: In the online deposit account

Interest earned:	$30,000 x 3.50% = $1050.00
Less tax	$1050 x .33 = $ 346.50
After Tax benefit	$ 703.50

Option 2: In your mortgage

Interest saved	$30,000 x 4.89% = $1,467.00
Less tax	0.00
After Tax benefit	$1,467.00

Interest savings are untaxed, so when compared to an income which is taxed, you wind up streets ahead (i.e. $1,467 in your pocket rather than $703.50). Break over, let's get back to it.

---

[1] If the debt is against a negatively geared investment property you're only ahead by the spread. Sadly your tax advantage evaporates.

The Savings Plan

Hopefully, you will have learned a bit about money management concepts before you started reading Mortgage Free, Debt Free. If you haven't, I highly recommend 'the barefoot investor' by Scott Pape, however you might as well finish reading Mortgage Free, Debt Free first.

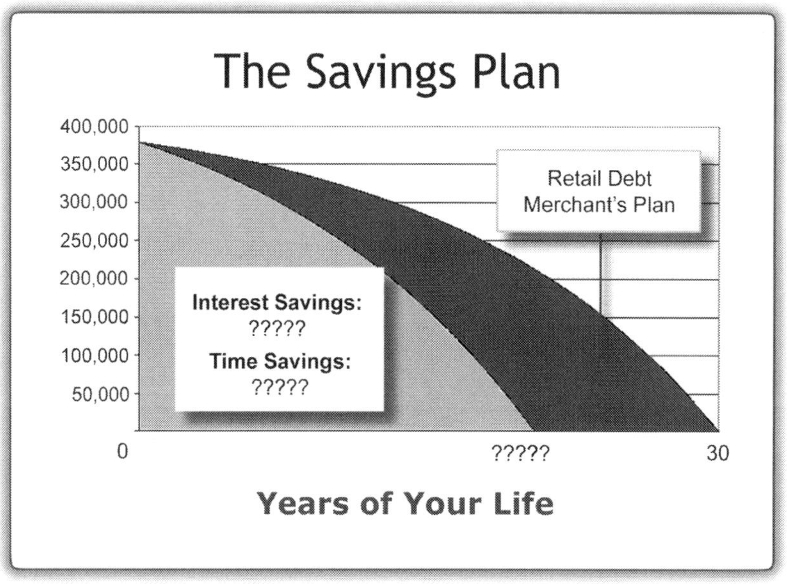

In barefoot, Scott talks about a recurring theme you'll hear from anyone wanting to help you get ahead - the importance of separating savings from spending money. Providing you understand these ideas, the Savings Plan strategy is the most effective, low risk way to reduce the cash and time it takes to pay off your mortgage.

All you need to do is treat your mortgage as your savings and goals account.

Unlike most of the other strategies, just how much faster you can smash your mortgage comes down to your own income, discipline and knowledge.

A quick refresher

In a world completely mad on credit, few people understand the difference between a "transaction account" and a "savings account". A transaction account is an account which you deposit and withdraw from both regularly and frequently. It's usually where your pay goes and where you pay your bills from. It often gets a hiding at the ATM or via a debit card.

Transaction accounts usually pay very little, if any interest, but offer ready, low cost/no cost access to your funds. Balances of these accounts usually hover at two tenths of three eighths of bugger all, so even if your bank was from some parallel universe where they paid incredibly high rates of interest you still wouldn't get much when it came to the dollars and cents of the thing.

Conversely, a savings account is an account where you regularly and frequently deposit money yet withdraw rarely.

The balance of your savings account grows steadily until your goal is achieved at which time you might make a withdrawal to pay for whatever it is you were saving for. Alternatively, perhaps your goals might have changed in the meantime and you will just leave your money sitting there.

It is usually simple to deposit money to a savings account, but withdrawing it may have limitations, fees or penalties. However the carrot is that banks often pay you increasingly higher interest as your balance grows. At the end of the year, you should have a nice balance, you will have earned (a little) interest which you will then be taxed on.

To achieve financial freedom, it is important to treat savings and expense money differently, to keep track of each separately. It's no accident that businesses use this exact approach.

How it works

As we learned a moment ago, the most effective savings account you have is your mortgage. Banks will always charge you more interest than they will pay you and you don't get taxed on interest that you don't pay. Your mortgage is already there so it SHOULDN'T cost you any extra fees either.

To make it work you must

Do it. Simply knowing that your mortgage is the most effective savings account isn't going to get you debt free any sooner. Going back to barefoot's advice, you need to make and implement a plan which should include savings for your other goals as well as mojo money for a rainy day.

Ease of use

This one's easy. How well it works is up to you.

Special Mortgage Features

- Your mortgage must accept extra payments (preferably unlimited).
- Your mortgage must allow redraw (preferably fee free).

Watch out for

Track your savings deposits to ensure you don't accidentally raid your mojo money when you reach your goal. Although your goal savings helps to reduce the interest you pay, it's the mojo money that does all the heavy lifting.

> If you end up taking a packaged loan, you can create separate loan accounts to simplify tracking of your different balances.
>
> Although you shouldn't have to pay extra fees to set them up or run them, they may attract individual fees when it comes time to close the loans down.
>
> If you're closing them because you are now debt free then who cares, but if you are closing them because it's time to move to a better lender then it could wind up costly, so beware.

Transactional Offset Strategy

Travelling under a range of names limited only by the imaginations of the merchants that pedal them, the Transactional Offset Strategy is the poor cousin of the Savings Plan. I use the word poor because it usually falls short on delivery when it's used as a stand alone interest saving strategy.

However get the right loan at the right price, bolt it to two or three of the other strategies and you might have yourself a bit of a goer.

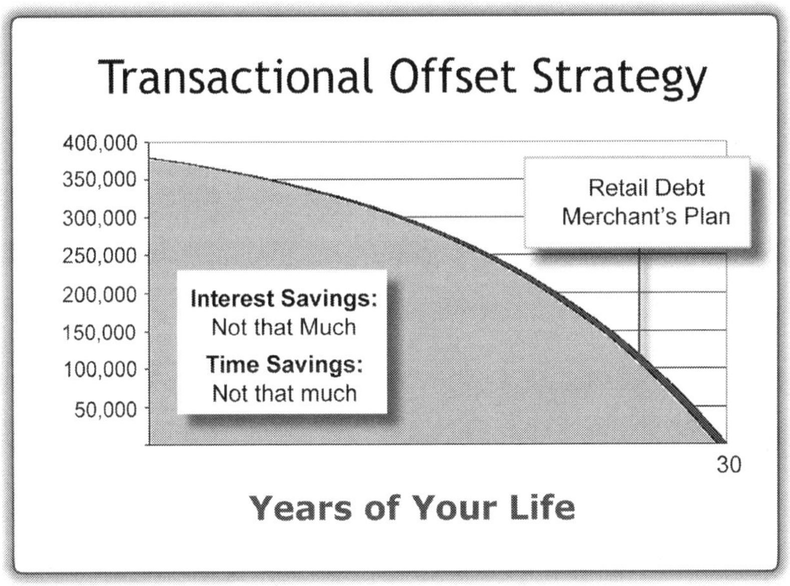

How it works

The Transactional Offset Strategy works by depositing every cent you earn into a mortgage offset account, then allocating that money out to your other accounts and needs from there.

An offset account is a Transaction Account which is separate to your actual loan, but linked only for the purposes of calculating the daily interest on your mortgage. Having $2,000 in your Offset Account has the same effect as having $2,000 deposited against your mortgage – you don't pay interest on it while it's there.

Whilst your mortgage replaces the need for a savings account, an Offset Account replaces the need for any transaction accounts. This should simplify management and reduce fees you would pay elsewhere.

The main advantage is that every cent in your offset account is working to reduce the interest and time taken to pay off your mortgage. Every day, 24 hours a day. Having said that, most people move money in and out of their transaction accounts so quickly, the interest offset savings are quite small when compared to the other four strategies.

To make it work you must

Get all your income deposited to your Offset Account and distribute the money from there.

You must also find the right loan type; paying VERY close attention to the notes in 'Watch out for' which is coming up.

Cancel your other transaction accounts.

Other than that, nothing much.

Ease of use

This really comes down to how well you select your mortgage and what facilities are available with the Offset Account.

Generally speaking, your Offset Account must allow you to do the things you already do in your everyday transaction account. Importantly, it should also fit how you see yourself using it as your main transaction account in the future.

Which facilities are most important when comparing Offset Accounts comes down to the things you want to be able to do with it. At minimum, a good Offset Account allows you to direct credit your salary, auto debit mortgage and credit card payments and Bpay your bills. Some may allow you to pre-schedule payments, others may not. What you want and what you get is up to you.

Special Mortgage Features

- Ummm... the mortgage needs to come with an Offset Account.

Watch out for

All in ones, Lines of credit or loans advertising 'offset', that do not have a separate offset account should be avoided. These types of loans combine all of your income and expenses into one account, making it difficult to track and manage your real progress. This can really hurt good interest savings from the most reliable strategies such as the Savings Plan, The +10 and The Free Money Strategy. Each of these strategies beat the interest savings of the Transactional Offset hands down so putting them at risk with any type of all-in-one loan is just plain silly.

Unfortunately, some lenders such as the Commonwealth Bank do not offer Transactional Offset accounts. The only alternative with lenders such as this is to create a small Line of credit or forget the Transactional Offset strategy altogether. Small means whatever the minimum for that lender is and NEVER more than $20,000.

Be very wary of any merchant suggesting you should take a large Line of credit to save interest or minimise debt. I have seen streams of failures using this approach and when interest savings don't appear, surprise, surprise, the merchants make more profit.

You should also keep your eyes peeled for transaction fees and charges, especially against services that you will use the most (i.e. eftpos or ATM withdrawals etc). Good Offset Accounts only have exception fees such as foreign ATM charges, dishonour fees and the like with all normal transactions being fee free.

And finally some offsets do not calculate on 100% of account balances which waters down any potential interest saving. These are called 'partial offsets' and while they are nice to have if the price is right and partial is all you can get, you should be able to do better.

The Free Money Strategy

My Mum always told me to save the best until last and as far as interest reduction strategies go, this is it. Although this strategy also has a number of different names, I like to call it The Free Money Strategy. That's Free Money as in getting money that doesn't cost you anything.

It's my favourite because it works. You set it up once, there's no maintenance and generally speaking, has no restriction on what other strategies, type of loan or features you choose.

With savings up to $57,000 on the average $379,000 mortgage and with no extra investment from you, what's not to love?

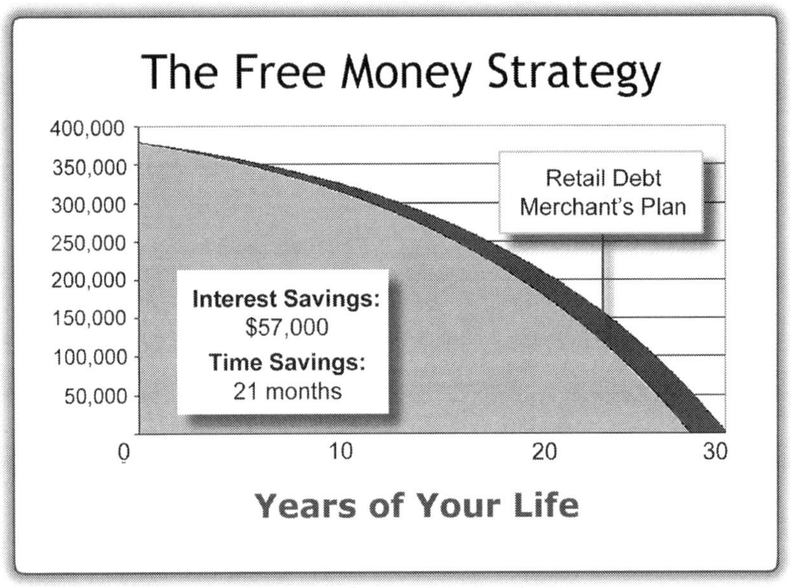

How it works

The Free Money Strategy taps into the fattest slice of the lender paid kickback pie. Trail commissions. The strategy boils down to two parts. Cashback deals and interest savings.

Now if that sounds a little technical, don't worry, it's actually very straight forward and incredibly safe.

1. Cashback Deals – payments made to you by your mortgage broker when they split their commission with you.

2. Interest Savings – the interest you won't pay by banking those extra payments against your loan and leaving them there to do good things.

Let's take a moment to understand the most controversial bit. The cashback deal. One of the greatest falsies doing the rounds is that mortgage brokers offer a value add service which is free. This is called a half truth as it is definitely true that good brokers offer a value add service, however it is not true that they do it for free.

Brokers appear free because they promote the same rates, repayments, fees and loans as the lender. If you go directly to that lender, they won't give you the commissions they would otherwise pay to the broker. Sure, the lender might offer you some token concessions to make you feel good, win the sale and cut the broker out, but they will also claw back extra profit for themselves along the way. They always do, so don't bother asking.

Instead, simply get your head around the fact that mortgage brokers charge lenders and lenders charge you. When there is no broker charging commission, your lender still charges you anyway. It's all about profit. The only question is whose wallet you want that profit to wind up in - your lenders, your brokers or yours.

The Free Money Strategy is about putting <u>that profit</u> in <u>your wallet</u>. It relies on trail commissions which in case the message still hasn't gotten through are the BIGGEST part of all commissions paid to your broker. These monthly kickbacks come directly from payments you make on your loan. They are the commissions that the industry wants us to ignore which is why they work so hard to play them down. They're pretty good at it too, because most consumers who know about trail commission payments don't think that they are worth much at all. Perhaps this is because it's not really talked about and IF you ever see anything disclosed about trail, it probably looks like this:

0.15% p.a.

Or it might be a bit more obvious, but somehow more meaningless like this:

Nil during the first year of your loan to 0.429% per

Don't forget what we learned in 'Objects in mirror are closer than they appear'. No matter how it is written, no matter what you are told, trail commissions which seem small aren't. They will make a massive difference to how much your mortgage costs you and how quickly you can get debt free.

To make it work you must

Forget about brokers touting cashback deals from upfront commissions and tap into trail commissions. Make sure you have them deposited directly into your loan account and leave them there forever.

Ease of use

Making sure you actually get 100% of the commission back is the trickiest part so pay close attention to the 'Watch out for' notes.

However once you set your loan up with a cashback broker, there's nothing else to do to make The Free Money Strategy work.

Special Mortgage Features

- Your mortgage must accept extra payments (preferably unlimited).
- The loan you want must be available from a cashback mortgage broker and lenders must pay trail commissions on that loan. Don't worry though, most loans from a

good range of lenders fall into this category, including the majors.

Watch out for

There are two types of commission brokers can pay to you as a cashback deal, the upfront commission and the trail commissions. Providing you have your loan for more than a few years, you will get more cashback from trail commission deals almost every time. Anyone telling you otherwise either expects you to refinance your loan every 3 years or so, or they are simply telling you porky pies. Either way, the information is a bit iffy.

You must take care when choosing a cashback mortgage broker ensuring all payments are based on 100% of the commission paid by the lender. Watch out for statements like "x% of what I get paid" or "y% of the broker's share". This is a clever way for brokers to sound like they are being generous while they quietly siphon off a chunk of commission through clever structures before they calculate your payment.

Don't choose your lender or loan based solely on how much commission it attracts. Getting the right loan must be your first priority as you will always wind up in front if you can get that same loan with a cashback deal regardless of commission rates. The $57,000 saving I have used is based on the average commission rates across most popular lenders, so while you could do worse, you could probably do better as well.

If you deploy The Free Money Strategy, make sure to read "Cashback Deals" which will help you source the right broker to maximise the benefits. Better still, get a professional borrower's agent to do it for you.

No matter what strategies you use, when interest rates fall, leave your repayment 'as is' and continue to live normally.

The extra cash will turbo charge the repayment of your loan.

“My problem lies in reconciling my gross habits with my net income.”
Errol Flynn

Revision: Choose your weapons

You have just learned about the most effective interest saving strategies to put your mortgage on the endangered species list.

You should now understand:

- ✓ Your mortgage must accept extra payments if you are to save interest and get debt free sooner.
- ✓ For most strategies, an offset account is optional ('O'), however if you can get one for FREE or for cheap, it can replace your everyday transaction account. This can save you on account keeping fees, but keep your eyes peeled for expensive transaction fees (like ATM charges).
- ✓ You don't pay interest on money you don't owe.
- ✓ The Free Money Strategy is the only way to save significant interest and accelerate loan repayment where <u>you</u> don't have to pay or do anything extra.

Strategy	*Savings*	*Extra Payments and Redraw*	*100% Transactional Offset Account*
The fortnight Payment Plan	$136,000	✓	O
The +10 Strategy	$154,000	✓	O
Savings Plan	?	✓	O
Transactional Offset	?	✓	✓
The Free Money Strategy	$57,000	✓	O

STEP 3

Design your debt

"Planning is bringing the future into the present so that you can do something about it now"
Alan Lakein

Now that you have decided which of the interest saving strategies you would like to apply, you have already begun designing the core structure of your mortgage.

The next thing to do is to bolt on the bits and pieces that will determine how safe you are from mortgage stress; whether you will waste money on the refinancing roundabout; how much your loan will interfere with your lifestyle and the maximum time it will take to repay your mortgage.

Risky Business

Risk is the likelihood of something happening. Impact is what you experience when it happens. Like it or not, risk and impact are present in every decision you make from the breakfast you eat to the features you take in your mortgage. Sometimes seemingly small or poorly considered decisions can expose you to moderately high risks and very high impacts. These impacts may take a little time to happen, but when they do the results can be devastating.

Although numbers are thinning, you probably know or knew someone who smokes cigarettes. In choosing to smoke, that person risks a slow, early, agonising death. Most of us, even smokers, consider this to be a VERY HIGH impact, yet people still smoke. This means that smokers are unaware of the risk; ignore it; believe the risk is low; or they consider the risk worthwhile. However, most educated non-smokers would think that adopting any of these beliefs is absurd, which is probably why they don't smoke.

> *"The real deal with property is being able to comfortably afford it"*
> *Scott Pape, the Barefoot Investor*

Of course the tobacco industry is one of the most heavily regulated industries in the world, yet that does little to protect smokers. Tobacconists sell cigarettes and tobacco companies play down the risk to your health because they make money selling tobacco products. They're merchants, their job is to sell. Imagine asking them whether you should smoke, what you should smoke and how often you should smoke.

The point is, while you should carefully mull over decisions that may impact your well-being there is never a right or wrong choice as much as a choice that feels right to you. After all, you're the one that ends up paying the price. Having said that, high impacts will probably affect those people closest to you and they will pay a price to some extent as well.

Be careful. Small decisions can have very large impacts.

The Unfun Rollercoaster

Interest rates go up. Interest rates go down. Small changes in interest rates on a large debt like your mortgage can put a big dent in your cash flow which is the money you live on every day. Small dents in your shiny, much loved lifestyle can be anywhere from a little inconvenient to downright stressful. Large dents can result in a complete lifestyle write-off, which, even after a long and costly repair, still leaves you damaged.

The good news is that getting your borrowing budget right can not only insulate you from a very scary ride, it can also put a much larger dent in that other thing you could live without. Your mortgage.

Without wanting to get all caught up in stuff you don't really want to know about, there is a really important concept that all borrowers should take a moment to understand. Australia has an independent central bank, known as the Reserve Bank of Australia (also known as the RBA or the Reserve). It's not a bank that you get your mortgage from, however it has an influence on the bank or non bank lender you get your mortgage from and seriously influences the interest rate you pay.

In normal circumstances, the RBA meets once a month, except January, to set an interest rate known as the Cash Rate Target. Although it has a number of other responsibilities and tools, the RBA uses the Cash Rate to turn the heat up or down on the economy with a plan of keeping inflation under control. Changes to the Cash Rate directly impact the interest rate of your variable rate mortgage.

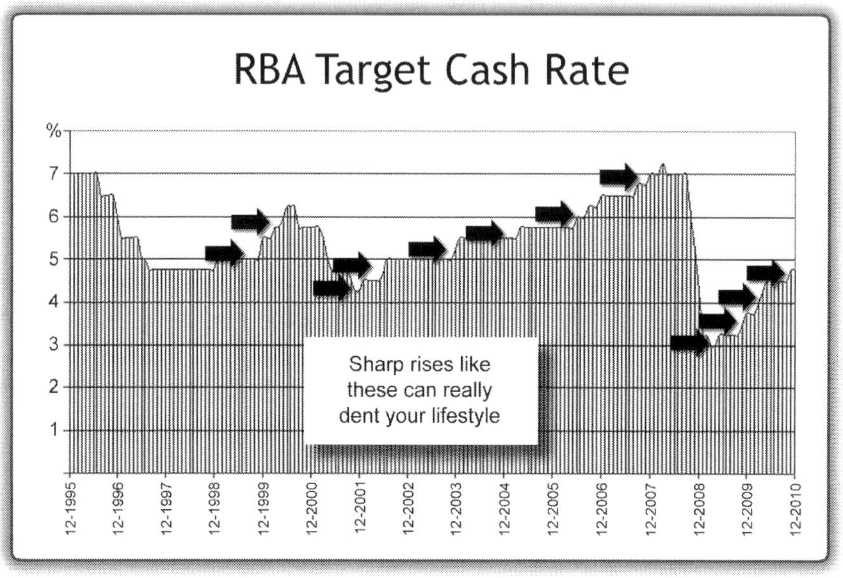

The movements in the Cash Rate Target set by the RBA in the 15 years between December 1995 and December 2010.

Glancing back over the last 15 years, you will see quite a big interest rate rollercoaster. Remember that changes to your interest rate directly affect your repayments, so you could think of this as a Repayment Rollercoaster. The peaks are where most people who suffer mortgage stress will really feel the heat, however for the last 15 years or so, those peaks have been relatively short lived. The highest Target Cash Rate over the last 15 years (the Peak Interest Rate) was reached in March 2008 and lasted for just one month. It then fell slightly, held steady for six months and before embarking on a rapid and record setting plummet in September 2008.

As you can see, interest rates in early 2009 were at record lows. Had you relied on those rates to guide your borrowing budget, you really would have felt the heat as they returned back to 'normal' levels. In a little over 18 months, your repayments would have increased by almost 50%. And they will go even higher at the next peak.

More importantly, in October 2007, lenders began turning their backs on the RBA by increasing their interest rates when the RBA chose to hold rates steady.

Since then, lenders have increased interest rates whenever they want and by however much they want. They have also refused to pass on rate cuts that the RBA delivers to the Cash Rate.

This adds a new dimension to the Repayment Rollercoaster. Now you can be sure to get a rate rise whenever the RBA announces one, but you can't be sure how much that increase will be. You also can never be sure that your lender won't change rates just because the RBA leaves the Cash Rate on hold, nor that you will see any rate cut even if the RBA takes a knife to the Cash Rate.

With that in mind, let's take a quick look at the most important principles in setting your budget.

To learn more about the RBA and what it does or to cure the most resistant case of insomnia, visit www.rba.gov.au

Setting your budget

Whenever I talk with someone about their mortgage, I always ask them one simple, yet most important question. "What's your budget?"

I cannot for the life of me remember anyone amongst the many thousands I have dealt with who didn't answer by telling me either the price of the property they want to buy, or the amount they think they need to borrow. (The latter then often blurs into a long and detailed explanation of their deposit and their understanding of the grants they may be entitled to or the duty they have to pay.)

Using a loan amount as your starting point creates a mindset where you magically 'fit' everything else into your budget. That might seem like a good idea in your head. In real life it's wedged somewhere between risky and stupid.

Imagine if you asked a renter what their budget is and they replied "Oh, I'd like to rent a house worth around $750,000, maybe a little more. But definitely not more than $800,000".

Although you may not be renting the house, by taking on a mortgage, you are renting the money. Unlike property rental which has strictly controlled limits on how often and how much rent can increase, no useful protection exists on rented money. Your lender can jack up the fees and the interest rate whenever they want. "What about fixed rates?" We'll talk about those in a moment, however no matter what rate type you take, when it comes to taking on debt, repayments must drive all borrowing decisions.

They are the bit that continues to affect you until your loan is fully repaid. Whether that affect is good or bad, a lot or a little, it starts right here.

Your repayments chew up your ability to live freely so setting a realistic budget for your weekly, fortnightly or monthly repayment is crucial. Get that wrong and your stress levels and the amount of money you spend on interest will be far higher than they need to be.

Or worse.

If you have already talked to a merchant about how much you can borrow, you hopefully discovered they are willing to lend you more than you want to borrow. A LOT more. If you find yourself in the situation where they will only lend you 'just enough' or worse, won't lend you enough, take a moment. Head to your nearest beach, park, forest or lake, take off your shoes, plant your bare feet in the earth and have a good hard think.

Lenders limit how much you can borrow based on your ability to meet repayments on a rate higher than current interest rates. This buffer is usually around 1-2% above the rate they charge you on day one. It is known as the Assessment Rate.

In the 2008 Global Financial Crisis, the RBA reduced interest rates to 'emergency levels' slashing the Cash Rate by 4.25% in just seven months. The RBA, the banks and the brokers all understood that in the medium term interest rates would return back to normal levels. Yet many debt merchants still slashed their Assessment Rates. This meant that even though your income might not have changed, the amount of money they would lend you went through the roof. It also meant that the safety buffer the Assessment Rate normally provides, which was probably already too small, became non-existent.

Debt merchants were pedalling mortgages they knew borrowers would struggle to repay as interest rates inevitably returned to normal levels well above their own Assessment Rates.

Merchants make money lending money. The more they lend the more they make.

If you go broke in the process, they've always got your property to sell and usually an insurance policy to cover shortfalls.

If there is a shortfall, you can be sued for that money, even if you paid a massive premium to the Insurer that's suing you.

For people interested in owning their property, living well and getting debt free as fast as possible, there's a better way to budget than asking a merchant how much you can borrow. To do this right, there are three 'formulas' you must understand:

Control = Comfort Zone *minus* Risk

Whether your goal is to motor along on minimum repayments or smashing it ASAP, maintaining control is crucial. Although you can never have absolute control, there is a simple rule that helps maximise it.

The rule is "maintain a healthy Comfort Zone".

Comfort Zone = Income *minus* Expenses *minus* Lifestyle

People with bigger comfort zones live more comfortable lives than people with big houses and small comfort zones. Sure, you can live a happy life and have a big house, however if your comfort zone is the size of a freckle on a gnats[1] bum, then you've got less to be happy about, or in the very least, less room to be comfortable.

The simple fact is that people with larger comfort zones have more to smile about, regardless of the amount of debt they have. They have more freedom in their lives and can get rid of debt faster wasting less money on interest and fees along the way. They can pick and choose the interest saving strategies AND afford to implement them comfortably. Whereas the only interest saving strategy that works every time regardless of your comfort zone is The Free Money Strategy.

There are three ways to improve your Comfort Zone:

1. Increase your income.

2. Reduce your general expenses.

3. Manage your Risk (i.e. your minimum repayments).

Repayments = Loan Amount *times* Rate *times* Term

Repayments are the centre of the mortgage universe. For most people, mortgage repayments are their largest single expense by a long shot. Get your repayment budget wrong and the best case is you will take years longer and pay thousands in extra interest. Worst case, you will pay even more again in fees and interest, be frequently stressed and you may face losing your home and your family.

The size of your minimum repayment is directly affected by how much you borrow, the loan term you take and the interest rate of your loan. Controlling your loan amount and loan term can help take some of the risk out of interest rate pressures.

No matter what you do, your interest rate will change over time. Rate changes are beyond your control and will cause your

---

[1] A gnat (say: nat) is one of a family of insects that includes flies and mosquitoes.

loan payments to change as well. Uncontrollable, increasing loan payments pose a risk to your comfort zone. The size of this risk depends on how well you set your repayment budget which is the amount that you plan to repay each week, fortnight or month.

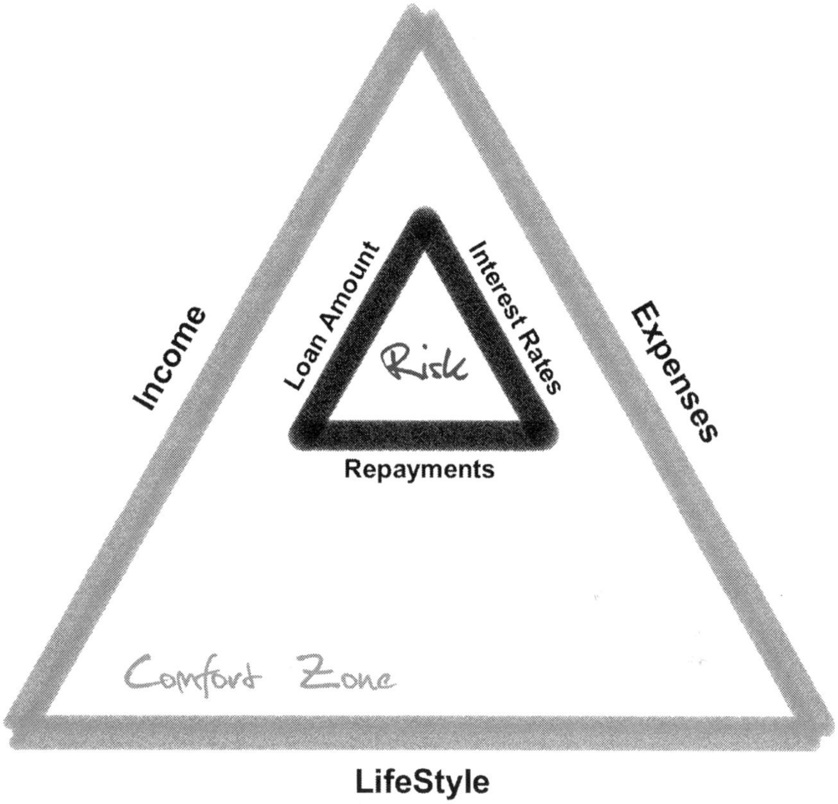

The larger your minimum repayment, the larger your risk. Your loan amount and loan term are the only things you can control that affects the size of your minimum repayment. Manage the amount you borrow and budget on a sensible rate to protect your comfort zone.

When setting your repayment budget, you should establish how much you can afford to spend on repayments before they begin to eat away at your comfort zone.

You must always set your repayment budget independent of what any merchant is willing to lend you or how much they are suggesting you should borrow.

When setting your repayment budget realistically consider:

- ✓ **Your Income:** What is your current income and how certain are you that it will continue at or above it's current level?

- ✓ **Your Life:** Make sure to plan your needs including rest and relaxation, holidays and whatever else melts your chocolate. If anything, having a big debt increases your need to take some time out, rather than reducing it.

- ✓ **New Expenses:** If your mortgage is to fund the purchase of a new property, don't forget to take into account extra insurances, rates, levies and other duties which could easily exceed $150 a month.

- ✓ **Family changes:** Will you, or do you have children? What are your changing needs? You might not have children now, but are you planning to within the time frame of your mortgage? Will you still be able to afford this loan losing one income coupled with your extra living expenses? (WHAT? Yes, babies and children will seriously mess with your budget on both the income and expenses side of the ledger).

- ✓ **Other goals:** If your mortgage is for an owner-occupied property, it's not so much an investment, as a long term savings plan that you can only cash in by downsizing. Make sure you allow enough headroom in your repayment budget to fund other financial goals.

Ultimately only YOU can decide how much you can afford to repay each week, fortnight or month.

As you budget your repayments, there are some important things to remember that you may or may not already know about.

WARNING:

Dangerously boring, but incredibly important reading for the next 2 pages.

Recommended Reading Time:
Between 9:30am and 11:30am after you have had your coffee and before you start to think about lunch.

How much should you borrow?

Unless you come into a windfall or sell your property, you will be living with your mortgage for many years. As we now understand, repayments during those years will increase and decrease completely at the discretion of your lender.

Never let a merchant set your repayment budget, loan term or your loan amount. Instead you should:

1. Set your own, comfortable repayment budget.
2. Work out your loan amount using the greater of the current interest rate or the Medium Term Rate.
3. Always allow and add a buffer to the rate.

Allowing a buffer for rate increases serves two benefits:

1. You can more easily accelerate repayment of your loan, becoming mortgage free sooner.
2. You can use that buffer to create a 'payments in advance pillow' cushioning you from inevitable rate movements, unexpected rate hikes or income problems.

A Medium Term Rate is an indicator based on historical interest rates over an extended period of time. Visit the KeyFacts web site to access the latest Medium Term Rate, Peak Interest Rate and repayment budget tools and tips that help you get it right.

A Practical Example

For example, assume you secure a variable rate mortgage for around 6.25% p.a. which on a $350,000 loan over 25 years requires you to repay $531 per week. The current Medium Term Interest Rate is 8.45% p.a. which means you should budget and make repayments at $645 per week – an extra payment of less than $17.00 a day.

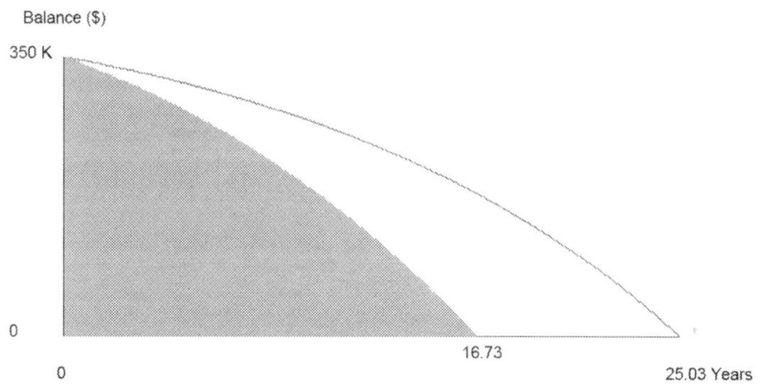

Although interest rates won't stay at 6.25% for long, if they did, you will be debt free more than 8 years faster and save $128,000 in interest.

Setting your budget sensibly allows you to stay ahead of the game. It helps keeps stress levels down and you can get debt free faster.

The greater the buffer you allow in your repayment budget, the safer you will be and the faster you will repay your debt.

The 1% Wonder

By now you may be feeling a little mathed out or ever so slightly overwhelmed by Peak Interest Rates, Medium Term Rates and other gobbledygook. Quite frankly, I don't blame you, so I thought that it might be time to introduce a really simple idea to help you budget for a mortgage you can kill in record time. It hardly involves any math, will save you interest, will radically shorten the time it takes to repay your loan and for the most part, iron out the bumps, peaks and troughs in the Repayment Rollercoaster.

It's called the 1% wonder because less than 1% of the people who read about it will ever actually do it AND 1% is the only number you really need to use. It follows the Keep It Simple Stupid principle and means you can totally ignore everything you just learned about Peak Interest Rates, Medium Term Interest Rates and worrying about working out comfort zones. Yay.

The 1% wonder has 5 simple steps:

1. Take the variable rate that the lender is charging you and add 1%. Let's call that the 'wonder rate'.
2. Calculate your repayment at the wonder rate using a 30 year term and set that as your repayment.
3. When the lender increases your rate, repeat steps 1 and 2. If you can't afford to increase the full 1%, don't, but do as much as you can. Relax, you've been building a buffer.
4. When your lender reduces your interest rate, leave your repayments where they are.
5. Do not redraw.

Doing the 1% Wonder on the average $379,000 loan when interest rates are 7.15% increases your weekly repayments by just $60. However it slashes your 30 year loan in twenty two and a half years, saving you over $156,000 in interest and seven more years in debt.

How safe are you?

If the 1% wonder doesn't thrill you, there's definitely still more budgeting work to be done. Plug your numbers into an online mortgage calculator and try a few different interest rates 2-3% higher than today's rate to help you see what happens as you ride the Repayment Rollercoaster.

> The calculator at www.keyfacts.com.au is free to use and automatically calculates your repayments based on an historical Peak Interest Rate (PIR) and the Medium Term Rate (MTR).
>
> Importantly, these Rates are updated regularly, so you always have access to the latest information.

If you are extremely comfortable with potential increases in repayments, then you can probably skip this section. However if your repayments seem like they could become challenging when interest rates jump up, you are risking mortgage stress. Your options are to:

1. Abandon the idea altogether (yeah, right).
2. Buy a cheaper property (umm, cross this one off the list if you have already bought the property and have a mortgage).
3. Get a bigger deposit by saving or putting the bite on friends and family (it MIGHT be too late to try this if you have already bought your property. Then again, don't ask, don't get).
4. Increase your income to enable you to manage a higher repayment.
5. Reduce your expenses to enable you to manage a higher repayment.
6. Buddy up.
7. Look into an Equity Finance Mortgage.
8. Screw it let's do it. Throw all caution to the wind, stick with your budget and hang on for one heck of a ride.

Options 1 – 5 are all really worthwhile considering, however they are also covered in a range of other books by people far more qualified and experienced than me, so let's stick to what I really know well.

Buddy Up

Whether you know it or not buying property with people other than your husband/wife/boyfriend/girlfriend/significant other is not that strange. In fact there is now a mortgage that actively encourages this idea. Where both owners once needed to be on the one loan, you can now buddy up while making separate loan applications and having separate loans.

Of course you don't have to stick with just this option as there are other products from various lenders that can also be customised to suit your needs.

Merchants never miss an opportunity to sell debt.

No matter what mortgage you go with, the thing to note here is this approach can get a little hairy so choose your partner/s carefully. Like all relationships, the things that can go wrong are only limited by each participant's imagination and capability. The more partners that are involved, the trickier it can potentially become.

While you might get into the market buying your dream property, have the protection of a sensible repayment budget and be punching away well at clearing the mortgage, your partner may not.

If you plan to be living together and have not already had some lengthy experience with this arrangement, you are also taking on a bit more risk. I'm not saying don't do it, I'm just saying think about it and be careful.

If you do find a mortgage mate, make sure you thrash out all the detail. Each of you MUST obtain <u>individual</u> legal advice.

Equity Finance Mortgage

An Equity Finance Mortgage or EFM[1] is like buddying up with a company that you don't know, rather than a person that you do.

The basic principle is that a company, let's call it your EFM buddy, takes a share in your property in return for funding that portion of the purchase under a long term, lump sum repayment agreement. This means you do not need to make any payments for your EFM buddy's share until you pay the loan out in full by either selling the property or refinancing it.

Strictly speaking, there is no actual interest charged, however your EFM buddy gets a slice of any capital gain on your property.

However you are restricted to using a controlled range of loans to purchase your share of the property and these may not be overly competitive. As a result, you are likely to pay higher interest on the 'traditional mortgage' you use to pay for your share.

Nonetheless, in combination with a traditional mortgage the merchants claim an EFM can be used to reduce your repayments by up to 25%. While this idea is worth looking into if it appeals, get the best legal advice you can before you sign anything. Also have a professional do some financial modelling so you know just how much money this product is likely to cost you BEFORE you make an application.

The idea is relatively new and is subject to an innovation patent. This means supply is restricted and somebody believes there is a lot of money to be made from it.

The good news is, you can use "The Free Money Strategy" with the controlled range of EFM loans on offer, so I guess that's something.

---

[1] EFM is a registered trademark of ARES Capital Management Pty Limited

Screw it let's do it

Sometimes things that make sense to adventurers like Richard Branson don't make that much sense to people like me. But that doesn't mean you shouldn't or won't do it.

Sir Richard bails near Hawaii. He was lucky to survive.

If this sounds like you and you are happy to take on a chunk of risk for the lure of a bigger reward then you should definitely have a good read of the next section. It could help make a potentially bumpy ride a little smoother.

Fix your mindset or your mortgage

In the case of rate type, you have a simple decision. Either you fix your interest rate, or you do not. Understanding and considering each alternative carefully is the only way you can make the right choice. Like all things mortgage related, the rate type needs to be your decision because you bear the impact.

If you don't fix, your interest rate will be variable. Your lender can change it either up or down, by as much as they like, any day of the week. Therein lays the risk of taking a variable rate mortgage.

The sixty four dollar questions are, will they, if so, by how much, when and for how long?

The answer of course is, buggered if I know. As we talked about in "The Unfun Rollercoaster", since October 2007, the factors influencing interest rates have changed. Up until that time, the interest rate on a variable rate mortgage moved largely in line with the 'state of the economy'.

When the economy was booming, employment would go up and wages would go up. So too would the interest rate on your variable rate mortgage, because that is when the RBA increased its Cash Rate. This made interest rate changes somewhat predictable and meant the historical risk and impact of a variable rate mortgage was relatively low. When interest rates rose, you were probably doing okay yourself and could comfortably cope with a bigger dent in your wallet.

However in October 2007, BankWest, now owned by the Commonwealth Bank, broke ranks and started moving their interest rates up, independent of the RBA. What started out as an unnoticed blip quickly became common practice for many lenders. ANZ was the first of the big four to try it, the Commonwealth Bank following not long after.

Each of the majors did it a second time and discovered that, although they got a bit of bad press, borrowers continued to flock to them and they still made gargantuan profits. So they did it again. And again. But this isn't about bashing the banks. Most of the building societies, credit unions and non bank lenders did it too.

Since that time, a bunch of other things have happened and lenders have become empowered and emboldened. They drive variable interest rates up whenever they feel like it and by as much as they want. They also refuse to pass on RBA rate cuts that in the past would have reduced your interest rate, winding back your financial pressure, or accelerating the rate you repay your loan.

So now, on top of the general economic triggers affecting interest rates, you must also deal with the practice of lenders striving to out profit each other by moving interest rates independent of the RBA. This increases the risk for anyone on a variable rate mortgage today, compared to someone on variable rate back when the banks toed the RBA line.

Nowadays, when interest rates rise, your ability to cope is less likely to keep pace and you may not be doing so okay yourself. Just as importantly, when the economy slows and mortgage rates should help you along by falling, your interest rate may just as easily stay where it is, fall by two tenths of bugger all, or perhaps worse yet, increase. As has been proven time and time again, lenders will always act to protect themselves, even if it is at your expense.

We need to think about the impact of this increased risk more carefully today than ever before. It is now far more likely to happen and when it does, you want to make sure you are prepared for it. What happens to your comfort zone if the lenders decide to increase rates another one or two percent above RBA recommendations?

If you followed the steps in "How much should you borrow?" the buffer you created on current interest rates means the ups and downs of the interest rate cycle should be quite manageable. Your comfort zone takes up the slack that your buffer can't during the top end of the rate cycle; then your buffer kicks the living daylights out of your debt at the bottom of the cycle, so you've got it made in the shade.

On the other hand if you've got one or more feet planted in the "Screw it let's do it" camp by budgeting repayments closer to current rates, you have probably left yourself little or no buffer for those ups and downs. Your journey will likely be a little longer, and quite a bit bumpier as you will suffer a greater impact each time the risk of increased interest rates becomes real. To some extent or another, it always does so if we can't fix your mindset, you might want to fix your loan.

A fixed rate is a loan with an interest rate that doesn't change for a certain period of time. This means your minimum repayments won't change either and this could help you stay in control. If you're not interested in fixing, it is still worth learning about these loans because this little bit of knowledge certainly can't hurt, whereas not having it certainly can. However whether you should actually take a fixed rate is an entirely different story.

In Australia the idea of a fixed rate mortgage is a little bit bullshit because in reality, there is no such thing. They probably should be called something like "Introductory Fixed Rate Variable Rate Mortgages".

While it's pretty obvious that I'm not the best person for product names, the point is that you cannot get a fixed rate that lasts for the full term of your loan. In fact the vast majority don't go past 5 years, which, unless you win Powerball, is a long way short of the typical loan term. So while you get some reprieve from the Repayment Rollercoaster with a fixed rate, it's relatively short lived.

In the past, with very few exceptions, taking a fixed rate has almost always cost borrowers more in interest and fees than taking the same loan on a variable rate. Which makes some people think "Screw it, why do it?" The answer is simple. Peace of mind. If you are thinking about fixing your interest rate then, "saving interest" is probably way down your list of priorities, somewhere below "sleeping well" and "keeping the farm".

A fixed rate mortgage is an insurance policy against financial pressure brought on by interest rate hikes. And for any kind of insurance you should always expect to pay a premium.

Fixed rate loans definitely do not suit everybody.

If you repay a fixed loan before the end of the fixed term, in full or for most lenders in part, you may have to pay Early Repayment Penalties.

Penalties can also be triggered if you switch to a different loan type during the fixed rate period even if you stay with the same lender.

Early Repayment Penalties can be MASSIVE and often vary from day to day. Although true for any mortgage, before taking a fixed rate term, make absolutely sure you fully understand the Early Repayment Penalties that may apply to you.

Most lenders can give you an estimate of an Early Repayment Penalty, but the actual cost will be determined on the day that the early repayment event occurs.

In the year between August 2007 and July 2008, interest rates on competitive variable rate mortgages rose by around 1.30% p.a. Many experts would have considered that increase unlikely. No matter what the risk actually was before it happened, it still happened. During this period, some borrowers raced to fix, others with more sensible repayment budgets rode it out, some stressed and survived and some people lost their homes. Each borrower experienced that rate hike differently and each suffered a different impact.

Some borrowers may also have taken fixed rates a few years earlier for temporary relief from the Repayment Rollercoaster. For many, those fixed rates were about to expire in the middle of a peak interest rate spike. No doubt those people, who paid a premium to be stress free for a time, were now feeling more than a little stressed.

However if borrowers were fixed during this entire period of higher interest rates, they would have been able to sit back laughing knowing both their lifestyle and property were safe. Of course smart borrowers who correctly set their repayment budget in the first place also managed the interest rate spike easily as their comfort zone and advance payments were taking up the slack.

The flipside to this is that in the following twelve months, interest rates plummeted at record speed to historic lows. Loans with rates close to 9% in August were now in the 5% range. Of course fixed rate borrowers had the certainty of being locked in at much higher interest rates and paying well over the odds. In the meantime, the smart borrowers kicked the living daylights out of their variable rate mortgages at record pace and wondered what all the fuss was about.

Taking a variable rate mortgage is a gamble.

Taking a fixed rate mortgage is gambling too.

You're just backing
the other team.

By all means look into taking a fixed rate with the knowledge that for a period you'll have certainty over repayment size, the lender you are stuck with and the interest you will pay. However you should also remember that certainty can still be stressful as well as costly.

Oh, and one more thing. If you are unsure whether to fix your rate or stay variable, merchants are likely to suggest a part-fixed and part-variable loan. The reassuring advice is 'you get the best of both worlds'. While it might sound tempting, it's the merchant that gets the best of both worlds, not you.

The fixed part, usually at a higher rate, anchors your whole loan with them no matter how well they look after you. It strips away your flexibility to vote with your feet. At the same time, if rates increase, your repayments also increase on the variable portion, stripping away repayment certainty, which is the only advantage of a fixed rate loan.

If you are still stuck in a land of indecision, consider staying variable, increasing your payments to slightly more than they would be if you took out a fixed rate loan today. Of course that might be a lot harder to do if you took the "Screw it let's do it" approach.

No matter what, now is not the time to make up your mind. Wait until you finish reading this book.

If you fix:

Make sure the rate is either locked or capped at the time of your application.

Locked means your rate is guaranteed not to increase prior to settlement. Capped means it won't increase, but if Fixed Rates fall, you will get the lower rate. There are usually time limits that apply to the length of the guarantee which will vary from lender to lender.

If you fail to 'lock' or 'cap' your rate, fixed rates could increase before your loan settles and you will be stuck for years on a rate that could be much higher than the interest rate you applied for.

Does interest only interest you

When it comes to mortgage payment options, you only have two - 'Principal and Interest' or 'Interest only'. Let's take a moment to understand some basic jargon and appreciate the difference between each of them.

- Principal is the money that you owe to your lender.
- Interest is the rent on the money that you owe to your lender.

A principal and interest repayment is where each time you make a payment, you repay some of your debt as well as the rent on the money that you owe.

Interest only is where each payment covers the rent only which means you will need to find some way to repay your debt later on.

As I mentioned back in "Blind leaps of faith", you may have heard that you can save money by paying interest only. You can't. Not ever. In reality, six things happen when you buy on an Interest Only basis:

1. You have more disposable income.
2. You pay more interest.
3. Merchants make more money from you.
4. You remain exposed to more risk for longer.
5. You rely solely on capital gain to increase your equity.
6. You cut off a golden parachute in times of emergency.

Of the six impacts that's five pretty negative outcomes. Although the idea that you can save money by paying interest only is a con, none of this automatically makes choosing interest only a bad thing if you are doing it for the right reasons. There are three of them.

Reason 1: You are paying interest only as damage control. This is important and I will cover it in detail later in the appropriately labelled "Part V: Damage Control".

Reason 2: Today's lifestyle means a lot more to you than how much it will cost you in the long term. This is definitely fair enough, however if you pay interest only because you are motivated entirely by your current lifestyle, Mortgage Free, Debt Free isn't going to be chock full of great news for you.

As a guide, payments on a $350,000 interest only loan at 7.15% per annum are about $64 a week lower while loan payments remain interest only. Although this might get you a bit of extra lifestyle today, doing it for just five years winds up costing you an extra $26,000 in interest.

Reason 3: The loan is for investment use and you have other personal debt or you plan to use the extra cash flow on other investments.

Paying interest only for this purpose can certainly help you achieve worthwhile financial gains <u>if</u> you use that extra disposable income wisely. The basic idea is that even though interest only costs you more on this loan, it enables you to make even greater savings or income somewhere else.

For example, if you have personal debt and an investment mortgage and your personal debt is charged at the same or higher interest rate, then paying interest only on your investment mortgage frees up cash to smash your personal debt faster.

Remember, all lenders and most mortgage brokers make more money if you buy on an interest only basis. Like many important features, merchants have a real conflict of interest advising you on the appropriateness of this feature for your situation.

If you are considering taking interest only, you really should talk with a professional accountant, professional investment adviser or a borrowers agent to get advice that lines your pockets, not your merchants.

Tweaking the term

You can typically take between 5 and 30 years to repay your mortgage and choosing your loan term is an important step in designing your debt. It helps prevent you from over borrowing and is an indicator of how likely you are to get mortgage free ahead of schedule.

If your natural inclination is to take the maximum loan term that you can get, then you are probably less likely to clear your mortgage ahead of schedule than someone who opts for a shorter term. It seems that people with the foresight and committed desire to get mortgage free faster, do, whereas people who shift debt elimination further down the list tend to lull in indebtedness. With a longer exposure to the pressures of the Repayment Rollercoaster plus the math behind how interest works, borrowers opting for a 30 year plus loan term have it stacked against them. Quite simply, you have to earn a LOT more money to repay the same debt.

Glance at any mortgage interest chart in this book, or anywhere else for that matter and you will notice they all have a curve in them. This curve happens because of the way your interest bill is calculated. It's called compound interest. Although most people understand that you pay more interest the longer you owe money, compound interest is a lot nastier than that.

In the simplest of terms I can think of, compound interest means you get a little less yet pay a lot more. If you double the time it takes to repay your mortgage you will MORE THAN DOUBLE your interest bill. Triple the time it takes to repay your debt and you pay more than triple your interest costs and so on.

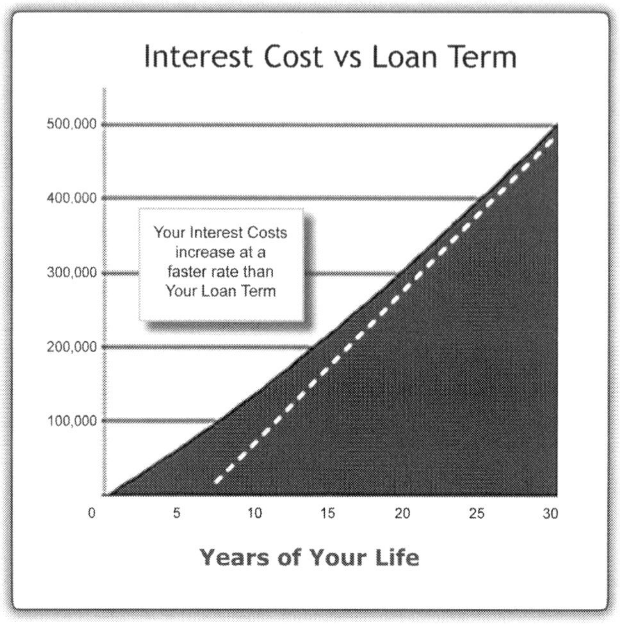

The steeper the line, the more rapidly costs increase. The dark area shows how interest costs increase over the longer term. You can see the slope between years 5 and 10 is less than that between years 20 and 25 when it really picks up. The dotted white line is one across for every one up, or 1:1.

Think about our average loan of $379,000 at an interest rate of 7.15%.

If you repay that debt in 10 years, you pay around $152,500 in interest which if you double is $305,000. Yet if you take double that time to pay it off (i.e. 20 years), you'll pay almost $334,500 in interest.

Take triple the time like many borrowers do, repay it over 30 years and the merchant charges you $542,500.

That's more than three and a half times the amount of interest you would pay if you killed the debt in 10 years.

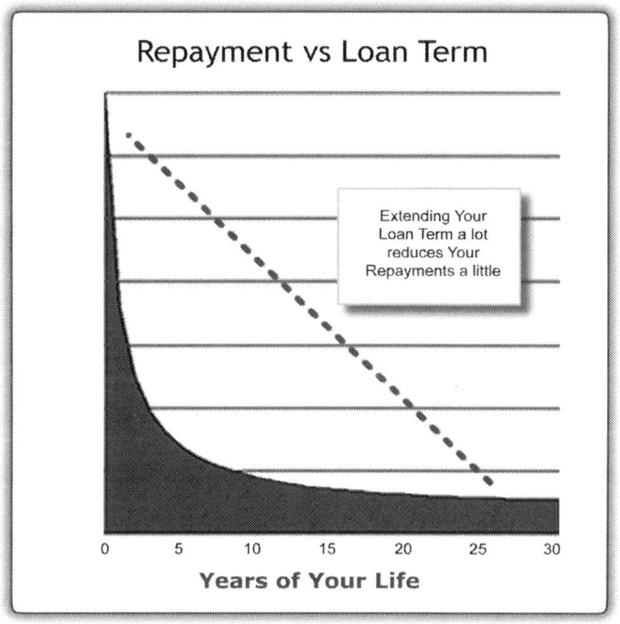

The steeper the line, the more rapidly your Minimum Repayments decrease. The dark area shows how repayments decrease when taking a longer term. You can see the slope between years 5 and 10 is far steeper than that between years 20 and 25 when it is almost flat.

The dotted line is one across for every one down, or 1:1. Compare this chart to the interest costs and you quickly realise you get very poor bang for your buck once you stretch the loan term beyond the 15-20 year mark.

The main thing to remember is taking a longer loan term reduces the minimum repayment you are required to make, however it also has a few serious problems.

1. You stay in debt longer.
2. You stay at risk for longer.
3. Small increases in loan term create:
    a. smaller reductions in minimum repayment
    b. much larger increases in interest costs

As a guide, you should always choose the shortest term that works for your comfort zone.

The following table demonstrates the impact that taking different loan terms can have for every $100,000 you borrow:

Term (years)	Minimum Weekly Repayment	Reduces Repayment by	Full Term Interest Cost	Extra Interest Cost
15	$210	-	$63,094	-
20	$181	$29	$88,045	$24,951
25	$166	$44	$114,736	$51,642
30	$156	$54	$142,988	$79,894

The above table is a guide to how much your Weekly Repayment reduces and the extra interest cost you will be charged when extending your loan term beyond 15 years per $100,000 borrowed. Calculations are based on an interest rate of 7.15% p.a.

Like interest only, both lenders and the mortgage brokers who keep trail commission make more money when you take a longer term, so they have a major conflict of interest when it comes to helping you with this feature.

Remember, you can readjust to a longer term further down the track if you find you have set your aim a little high. This is called re-amortising your loan and can be arranged with a simple call to your lender.

But before you do that, you should make sure you read "Part V: Damage Control".

Things you might not know you need

Okay, so far we have discussed and thought about different aspects of your loan to get it to fit you just right both now and into the foreseeable future.

However if you want to avoid getting caught on the refinancing roundabout, there are some other features you really should make sure are available in your loan. It's pretty fair to say that most loans WILL have these features, but not all so I would like to take some time to help you understand what these features are, why or when you might need them and how they work. Then you can decide for yourself whether they're important to you.

Why you must consider these features

Although I am far from the world's greatest fan of polls, surveys and statistics, like most, I'm happy to fling them out there when they support my ideas or point of view. So here goes.

There's a business which you probably haven't really heard of called Fujitsu Consulting that does quite a bit of work studying the mortgage and finance industry. In fact lenders and the MFAA alike retain Fujitsu to collect, crunch and analyse masses of mostly mundane facts. Fujitsu, in conjunction with JP Morgan has for the last few years, produced a publicly accessible report called the "Australian Mortgage Industry". Packed full of interesting statistics for the avid mortgage data junkie with too much time on their hands (i.e. me), the one that everyone taking out a mortgage should really think about is the 'reasons people refinance' statistic. Why? Because refinancing always costs you time and always costs you money. Always.

When you refinance, you might write off a little, say $300 if you stay with your existing lender, or a lot if your refinance decision includes switching lenders as well. I can't tell you just how much 'a lot' is likely to be as I have seen cases where refinance costs topped $35,000 with break fees and lenders mortgage insurance. Really, the sky is the limit and the financial damage is individual.

Regardless, my point is that refinancing is costly, so if you can avoid it by getting your loan right in the first place, you should.

According to the Australian Mortgage Industry report the reasons that 90% plus of mortgages are refinanced can be clustered into five categories:

1. To purchase a car; a boat; or pay for a holiday;
2. To invest in the stock market;
3. To invest in property;
4. To consolidate debt;
5. To reduce monthly repayments.

These categories are absolutely consistent with the masses of borrowers who I have interviewed to discuss refinancing over the years. Without getting into the pros and cons of each reason, they can be grouped into two simpler needs:

1. To access existing equity in property; or
2. To reduce monthly commitments.

So if we set the features to allow us to meet both of these needs in your next loan, we reduce around 90% of the reason you would need to spend time and money on a costly, external refinance.

When you are likely to need these features

There's another statistic that Fujitsu calculates, but doesn't publish in this report. That's the one called the 'average life of a mortgage relationship'. In layman's terms 'average life of a mortgage relationship' is the average time it takes for a loan to be paid out. Of course the reality is that this statistic is impossible to calculate accurately which is probably why it isn't published in the report in the first place. It just sort of floats around the media and the industry as some sort of Chinese whisper. Nonetheless, in March 2010, Fujitsu told me this average is 6.2 years.

Unlike the "reasons people refinance", the statistic suggesting you would pay out your loan every 6.2 years is completely inconsistent with the people I have interviewed. However my experience is based on borrowers with the right features built into their loan in the first place and who were also given the right information at the time they were contemplating a refinance decision.

Of course the Fujitsu average might simply be pointing out that many borrowers seek refinance help from debt merchants whose job it is to sell new debt. Fortunately, we're on to them and all we have to do is understand what features you need; why you might need them; when you might need them and how you could use them.

Features to access existing equity in property

Let's start by addressing the most common reason to refinance and perhaps the simplest one to solve, "To access existing equity in property".

Top Ups

All you need here is to ensure your loan allows Top Ups. Although the fees and definition for Top Ups may vary a little from lender to lender, the principle is that you can request a return to your original loan limit for a nominal fee and without having to jump through the hurdles of a new application. At the time I wrote this book (2008 - 2011) and for the ten or so years prior, you would expect this fee to be around $300 or so. Top Ups work like this:

You originally borrow $379,000 and make minimum principal and interest repayments on your 30 year loan each month. Five years on and you will have paid about $32,000 off, making your loan balance somewhere around $347,000.

Activating a Top Up offers quick access to that $32,000 for a once off fee at the lower end of the scale. Most commonly your loan term doesn't change and this means that your repayments will increase slightly. These higher repayments help keep your interest costs down and ensure that you stay on track to becoming mortgage free sooner. They are a small price to remind you that you have taken a backward step.

Even though this could be the most effective way to access your equity, remember that you are still costing yourself money and making it harder to become mortgage free. Make sure you use that money well - ideally to make more money to accelerate the repayment of your debt.

Features to reduce monthly commitments

I have to start this section by re-iterating that reducing your repayments by even a small amount radically increases the money and time it will take you to become mortgage free. However, it's also fair to say that from time to time, you may need to make temporary changes to deal with shifting circumstances.

Let's face it, life is dynamic and at times, unpredictable.

Interest Only

Back in "Blind leaps of faith" you read my warning against the costs of paying interest only. I won't try to hide that I am biased against interest only, but that's strictly because of the way some merchants sell the feature without explaining the costs and risks.

While you should take your mortgage on a principal and interest basis, it is extremely worthwhile to ensure that you can easily switch it to interest only. You may need it later on to alleviate short lived mortgage stress and can learn more about this strategy in "Part V: Damage Control".

Taking a quick look at the example loan in "Top Ups" and assuming your rate was 7.15% per annum, you could reduce your monthly principal and interest repayment from $2,559 down to $2,062 interest only. That frees up almost $500 a month. Remember, this is a reduction in repayments which makes it a long term cost, not a saving.

We won't talk about how much it costs you because you already know it's ugly.

Re-amortisation

I have included re-amortisation not because I think it's a good idea, simply because I get asked about it quite a bit. Personally, I think re-amortisation is a big dud and something you should always avoid doing at all times and at all costs.

Re-amortisation is when you restart your repayment clock, extending the time you have to repay your debt, which then lowers your repayments. Re-amortisation only applies to principal and interest loans so if you have opted for interest only you can skip this feature. It won't help you.

Taking a quick look at the example used in "Top Ups", re-amortising your remaining 25 year loan term back to 30 years will reduce your monthly repayments by around $220, which isn't a great deal on any level. However if things are that bad, well…

Remember, this small amount of relief comes at great cost in the long term. That's great as in massive, not great as in fantastic. Re-amortisation really is a last resort and should be avoided unless the only alternative is a life of misery. Still, it's nice to have as many options up your sleeve as you can, if you ever find yourself in hot water.

Splits

Mention the word split to most people and they immediately think part fixed, part variable. Splitting simply means dividing your loan amount across more than one loan facility. Each loan can be exactly the same type of facility, have a minor twist or be completely different.

For example, we just took a look at using Top Ups as a quick and easy way to access $32,000. If your loan is on your home and you plan to use the Top Up to pay for a holiday or non-investment use then you would probably choose to simply Top Up your existing loan and would ignore splits altogether.

However if you are planning to use the Top Up as a deposit on a rental property or to purchase some other investment, the costs of establishing the facility and the interest cost associated with that debt may be tax deductible. Your owner occupied loan is not.

If your loan has the ability to split, then you can simply have the Top Up established as an Investment Purpose split to simplify your annual tax returns. You could also make this split interest only to allow you to prioritise repayment of your non-deductible, personal debt. Of course you don't HAVE to make this a separate split and your accountant is the best person to talk to about this. I shouldn't have to remind you to do this before you borrow the extra money. Doing it afterwards is a little late.

Being able to add splits can also come in handy if you ever find yourself needing to consolidate other debt. I'll explain the best way to do that later.

You may not need any of these features today but at least you now know why you might need them at some point down the line. It pays to factor these features into your thinking as they could help you avoid unexpected wastage of time and money if the unexpected happens to you.

Ultimately whether you decide your mortgage 'must have' any of these features is up to you; however experience says you really should factor these features into your ideal mortgage.

Cross collateralisation

If you have more than one property, then you should learn about cross collateralisation. If not, then feel free to skip ahead.

People sometimes get cross collateralisation mixed up with having several loans, which may or may not involve several properties with one lender. It's not.

Cross collateralisation, also known as cross securitisation is when you pool multiple properties and this pool is then treated by the lender as a single security.

For some borrowers cross collateralising is a good thing, for others, it's a bad thing.

The only justifiable reason to cross collateralise is to save money by avoiding or reducing an LMI premium. However depending on your circumstances this may be a significant financial incentive.

On the other hand, the reasons you may not want to cross-collateralise can easily outweigh this benefit too. They include:

- You are a risky borrower and are likely to fall behind in loan repayments.

  If you fall behind on loan repayments for one loan, your lender may foreclose against all of your properties. However in most cases this can be avoided with early action and negotiation.

- You make frequent changes to your loan limits, or properties.

  Each time you do, your lender may require you to revalue all properties in the pool.

  It can be costly and time consuming to make changes but that's probably not the showstopper.

  Cross collateralisation is a real problem if a property valuation comes in below expectation, especially if you are already financed to the eyeballs.

  A lower than expected valuation can stop you from accessing equity in other properties. It can also prevent you from making changes to your portfolio such as selling off properties or expose you to paying big LMI bills that you could otherwise have avoided.

The riskier you or your strategy is, the more likely it is that you should avoid cross collateralisation.

While cross collateralisation is mostly harmless to conservative investors, it could turn a highly geared 'property portfolio' into a house of cards.

Like many aspects of mortgage and finance, merchants can play both sides of the fence to get the result that works for them. You need to decide for yourself whether cross collateralisation works for yourself. If you need more help making this decision, pay a professional, non-commissioned adviser to help you work out the right answer for you.

> If you have more than one loan, keeping them with one lender can be done without cross collateralisation. This gives you increased buying power when it comes to getting fee waivers and interest rate discounts.
>
> It can also simplify your every day management of your loans and help produce more positive answers when you are asking for help.

Revision: Design your debt

Forget 'are we there yet' and start asking 'are we here already?' Getting the right structure is a critical step to mastering your mortgage and believe it or not, you've got the core bits down pat.

You now have all the information to design a mortgage which you can (a) live with and (b) get rid of as soon as possible.

You should now understand that:

- ✓ Your comfort zone protects your lifestyle.
- ✓ Your minimum required repayment affects your comfort zone.
- ✓ Interest rates affect your minimum required repayment.
- ✓ Interest rates will go up and down.
- ✓ Fixed rates can provide some insurance.
- ✓ Interest only lowers repayments but increases interest costs.
- ✓ Taking a longer loan term can provide some buffer.
- ✓ Increasing your loan term a little increases your costs a lot.
- ✓ There are four features you may not need today that could save you a lot of time and money refinancing in the future.

With that all done and now that you know what you need, let's learn how to get it.

STEP 4

Turning the tables

"I love to go shopping. I love to freak out salespeople. They ask me if they can help me, and I say, "Have you got anything I'd like?" Then they ask me what size I need, and I say, "Extra medium."
Stephen Wright

You may not have realised it, however you have now compiled your own picture of your perfect mortgage structure. All the key elements should be taking shape in your head.

What interest saving features you want and how you plan to use them; how much you want to borrow; what the maximum time is you would like to repay your loan; how risk works and how much you are willing to take on; and whether you should fix your loan.

By now you should also have a solid sense that, without the inside straight, the mortgage sales game has been stacked against you. With a better understanding of what you need, let's learn how you will get it.

Let's go shopping.

Hang on a minute

My mum used to tell me that a stitch in time saves nine. Although I have never been into sewing, I have found that a little extra time invested in getting things right can head off a lot of costly rework later on.

Take the time to shop properly, choose the right mortgage and you will only ever have to do it once, or maybe twice. Cut corners, let the merchant own the expedition and you risk screwing up one of the most important financial decisions of your life. You may have to refinance it four, five or six times over like those poor folks surveyed by Fujitsu, who pay out their loans every 6.2 years on average. Of course you will also probably spend many wasted years working to pay off the extra cost of these dumb decisions.

Take the time to invest yourself into the process of choosing a loan. Own the experience and don't let any merchant tell you they know more about what you need than you do.

Your money or your life

When it comes to shopping your loan, you will always be faced with making some choice between your time and your money. Investing more of your time learning, comparing and making sure you've got the right loan can definitely save you money. Investing your money to pay a professional who acts on your behalf will definitely save you time. Get the right one and it should also save you money and stress.

So let's take a quick look at the different ways to shop your loan.

Do It Yourself

This is a tried and tested approach that gives you maximum control, maximum range and up until late last century, Do It Yourself was the only option you had. Although the DIY option is still available, the mortgage landscape has become a lot more complex. As we've discovered, the merchants that charter these lands everyday know exactly what it takes to sell to you. Nonetheless, DIY is still a popular choice.

Almost every person who chooses to DIY spends more time in selecting and arranging a loan than someone who takes professional advice. They also commonly spend more money on their mortgage over the medium to longer term. A lot more. Nevertheless let's take a moment to think about what's involved.

The starting point is choosing lenders that you intend to approach. Assuming you want to get a pretty competitive deal if not the prize loan, you will need to do a little research.

It probably sounds crazy; however I'm yet to find a near complete list of lenders offering the ordinary borrower a reasonable mortgage. This means you can forget finding a complete list of products they offer, what their rates are or what nasty little fine print lurks beneath their clever marketing. For now at least, a reliable, detailed list just doesn't exist.

Taking a fairly wild guess there are probably around 180 or so lenders out there. Actually, that's more of a rough guess than a totally wild one. This number is based on the list of banks, building societies and credit unions that the Australian Prudential Regulatory Authority has authorised to take deposits. That currently numbers 178; however some of those businesses don't offer mortgages.

On the other hand, originators that might offer you a mortgage such as MyRate, Resi, Aussie and Mortgage Ezy just to name a few, aren't on that list.

Assuming that 180 is a realistic number of lenders selling mortgages, that each of those lenders offers two products which could fit you quite well, and allowing 90 minutes per product to conduct manual research and analysis (*faster* than I can do it), it will take 22.5 days to work out the best mortgage for you.

This of course, is utterly ridiculous and the only sensible option is to make a shortlist. The question is how do you know you aren't crossing off winning lenders? The answer is that you don't. It's pot luck. However there are some steps you can take to improve your odds.

1. Shop as many lenders as you can manage. The more time you are willing to invest in this activity, the better your pool of lenders will be, because quite simply, your pool will be larger.

2. Make sure to get at least two lenders that are:

    a. Major Banks. (ANZ, CBA, NAB and Westpac.)

    b. Regional/Minor Banks.

    c. Building Societies and Credit Unions.

    d. Mortgage Originators.

3. Never ask a merchant for their opinion of either themselves or different lenders.

4. Only choose lenders you are happy to deal with.

Now I know point 4 is a little obvious, however you would be surprised at the number of borrowers I have spoken with who wound up with a crappy loan and at some point in the conversation said to me "I knew I shouldn't have..."

At this stage, don't try to choose your lender based on features, fees, interest rates or any other measure calculated or paid for by the merchant (i.e. star ratings). You should also ignore awards unless you actually sat on the judging panel which only otherwise included borrowers agents and where your scenario was used as the test case.

You then need to get objective quotes from any lender that you feel is seriously in the running for your business. I'll explain the simple and most effective way to do this in a moment.

Use a mortgage broker

Without doubt the fastest way to create a shortlist of lenders is to turn to a mortgage broker because they only deal with lenders willing to fork out commission. However an unknown factor is just how short that shortlist really is.

No matter how you choose to shop, with so many lenders, brokers and loan choices, you need to narrow your search to a short list that feels right to you.

Although many mortgage brokers claim to have 40 or more lenders, when you put that to the test, this typically falls to 15 mainstream lenders or less. The rest of their 'panel' is often stuffed with non-conforming, obscure or commercial lenders and some others offering different finance products such as deposit bonds, personal loans and hire purchase. Brokerages may also advertise a number of lenders as being a part of their 'panel' that your individual broker may not be authorised to deal with – yep that's legal. This probably explains why Fujitsu's survey of mortgage brokers found that 11% of brokers actually used just two lenders or less and a startling 62% used four lenders or less.

Like it or lump it, there is no real way for you to test just how many lenders your broker will actually be able to help you with, however according to Fujitsu, it's the odds on favourite to be 4 lenders or less.

While it's fair to say the Fujitsu report, which was published in November 2006 did not sample every broker; Fujitsu considered it a large enough sample to warrant publishing its report. Perhaps more importantly, the pressure for mortgage brokers to look after a select few lenders has increased significantly since the survey. Differences in commissions paid by lenders have really widened creating more commission pressure from different lenders than ever before. Brokers that can turn the cheek to commission pressure are now faced by lenders requirements to maintain minimum volumes. In simple terms, send us some loans broker, or we cut you off. Ouch.

Finally, there are the silent incentives, like easy approvals, quicker turn around times and smoother settlements. These might sound like things that benefit you, however a key promise your broker makes is that they will do all the legwork for you. If your broker doesn't have a sales team as well as a separate team looking after settlements, they lose valuable selling time approving and settling your mortgage. An easier ride for your broker makes it easier for them to do less yet earn more.

That's not to say you shouldn't use a mortgage broker, you just need to be aware that shortcuts and easy rides, commission pressures and volume hurdles benefit your broker, not you. If you understand this, then you will also understand that you never really know whether the broker is putting you first or their own hip pocket. It's just a matter of taking a blind leap of faith…

The good news is that like the DIY route, you can request quotes that deliver better information so you still own the decision without adding cost or complexity. Stay tuned, you're almost there.

Hire a professional adviser

A borrower's agent is a qualified mortgage professional equipped with the right tools, connections and know how to advise and guide you to getting the right solution for your needs. It's not to say that mortgage brokers aren't professional, it's just that they are professional salespeople paid by the lender, not professional advisers paid by their clients.

On the other hand, borrower's agents are professional advisers who do not suffer any conflict of interest. Unlike any merchant, a borrower's agent works exclusively for you. Their lender range and services are limited only by your budget and desire to get it right.

More than simply guiding loan selection, borrower's agents can help you implement important strategies such as "The Free Money Strategy" and "The +10". Practical strategies to help you get mortgage free that merchants simply won't talk about because they cut into their profit. Your agent can also advise whether advanced strategies such as "Sweep to save" are likely to help or harm you as well as helping implement them if it's appropriate.

As a general rule, borrower's agents will compare far more lenders than you will find on any mortgage broker's panel – that's more in depth, quantity and quality. Unlike brokers, there is no reliance on commission and unlike the smiling faces at the local branch; borrower's agents only have one person to serve. You.

The fee to 'advise'; 'compare and advise'; or 'compare, advise and arrange' will vary depending on the complexity of your needs, the agent you choose and how far you go in the process.

Unlike merchants, a borrower's agent has a clear and defined responsibility to tell you if you are not ready for a mortgage; if they think you are borrowing too much as well as which deals really are the most ideal for you no matter which merchant is offering it. They are not subject to volume hurdles, commission pressures and soft incentives.

As a rule, you should have your borrower's agent compare as many lenders as your budget allows. Ideally this will be as many as you would compare yourself if you had the time, tools and experience to do it. Initial rankings should take in at least 15 mainstream lenders including cashback deals on offer from the leading players. Strictly speaking there is no limit to the number of lenders any one agent compares. Having said that, even with the best professional software and the latest lender information, researching the whole market will be very time consuming.

When it comes to professionals, time = money. I expect the dollars you spend on a whole of market approach will cost you more than it is ever likely to save you. At least in today's market.

Nonetheless, the price of using a good borrowers agent will return tenfold for most people and it is usually better to pay a little today than risk a lot tomorrow. I urge you to at least think about it.

Use a Pro-Consumer Agreement

If you are having trouble tracking down a borrower's agent that meets your needs, don't panic. The next best thing could be to hire a mortgage broker using a Pro-Consumer Agreement (a "PCA"). As explained earlier, a PCA is when you engage a mortgage broker for an agreed fee which can be a fixed amount or an hourly rate that covers the cost of your broker's service. In exchange, the broker provides their regular help then rebates 100% of all commissions to your loan. This ensures commissions cannot get in the way of their advice and is another way to implement the Free Money Strategy.

Although this idea isn't openly promoted by brokers there are definitely a number of professionals that have a preference for it. This means you can approach any mortgage broker to work under a Pro-Consumer Agreement which gives you more choice amongst advisers until borrower's agent numbers grow.

> *"I would much prefer an upfront fee."*
> *John Symond – Aussie Mortgage Brokers*

Although you might fork out less money upfront using a PCA over a borrower's agent, it is important to remember that you're still left with the limited lender range of ordinary mortgage brokers. And remember, that could mean that they shop fewer lenders than you have thumbs. There is little doubt that you are more likely to get a much larger range of lenders and products by dealing with a dedicated borrower's agent, so take a moment to find one if you can. Otherwise, things to watch when hiring a broker on a PCA include:

1. If your broker provides support on everything from choosing your loan right through to settlement, you should expect to pay them around $2,500 or so as a guide. That's an allowance of ten hours work at $250 per hour. This might sound like a lot, however the cash you get back from the upfront commission should go a long way to covering this cost almost immediately. The benefit from any trail commission will also continue to grow helping you to get mortgage free, debt free faster.

2. If you want your broker to come to your home, you can expect to add $500 to $1,000 to cover the cost of their travel. While the face to face might give you a warm fuzzy feeling, it doesn't guarantee a better standard of advice or service. Personally, I doubt it's worth it.

3. Forget percentage driven payments. A larger loan amount doesn't mean more work for the broker. Worse still, payments based on loan size leaves brokers open to encouraging you to borrow more so they earn more.

4. Watch out for 'fee for service mortgage brokers' aka cake pigs. A growing number of brokers want to eat their cake and have it too. If they charge you a fee, they should sign a PCA and give you the commission.

5. Download and use the Pro-Consumer Agreement from www.proconsumer.com.au for maximum protection.

If using a Pro-Consumer Agreement, make sure you pay special attention to "Cashback Deals" later in this book. Remember that your mortgage broker should pass back 100% of all lender commissions including both upfront commission and the trails.

Go to www.proconsumer.com.au to access free templates and find businesses that put your interests before commissions or to just locate a borrower's agent jump online at www.borrowersagent.org.

What is good value?

Whether you DIY, use an ordinary mortgage broker, hire a broker using a Pro-Consumer Agreement or hire a borrowers agent, you will still be faced with quite a few decisions. Although you may be able to rely on the opinions of others, you're the one that wears the cost of bad choices or reaps the benefit of good ones. So what can you use to reliably measure the value you will get from one loan, lender or feature, over another? Let's start by taking a gander at what most borrowers use... Rate.

Lenders have for many years been training their sales people, the media and borrowers to compare on rate, so most of us automatically do. You'll see references to interest rates everywhere. In advertising; in the paper; on the 'you beaut' loan comparison software and mortgage advertising sites across the internet. But what on earth are you really looking at?

You already know the Advertised Comparison Rate is quite useless but there is a litany of other interest rates you might see like:

- Nominal Rate
- Annual Percentage Rate (APR)
- True Rate
- Effective Rate
- Average Annual Percentage Rate (AAPR)
- Headline Rate
- Start Rate
- and more…

Although merchants may argue the benefits of one standard over the other, these rates do not share a rigid definition or standard formula. Even if they did, you just can't forget GIGO.

Assuming any of these rates is vaguely accurate for your situation (which is a really BIG assumption), how do you know whether the mortgage you are about to buy is good value? The answer is, most people don't.

Over many years, I have asked a lot of borrowers "Is your mortgage good value?", yet I have never had one person reply with a confident "yes". Answers typically range from "I don't know" through to "I guess" and my personal favourite "what's good value?"

Nonetheless, once I have any answer, I ask "How much does your mortgage cost you?"

This question is usually met with a puzzled expression before some tell me an interest rate; others tell me what they "think" their repayment is and some tell me the discount they got.

No-one has ever told me even roughly what they thought their mortgage will cost them over the next one, two, five, seven or thirty years. No-one has ever mentioned a dollar figure. Ever. Yet when I ask how much their house cost them, they'd tell me the exact price in a heart beat. If I asked whether that house was good value, they would immediately tell me whether it was or wasn't, whether they paid too much, or whether they got a steal. Most could tell me what made their property good value and the prices and features of other houses they had compared which helped them understand the value of the one they bought.

That's because when we buy most things, we know just how much top of the line will cost, what it will include for that extra money; how much we'll spend on the middle of the road product; what we'll miss for taking the cheapest deal and how much money sacrificing those features will save us.

Value is subjective, however broadly speaking even when it comes to your mortgage, value is defined by how much you pay for it and how well it does what you need it to do. Although there are a few exceptions, any mortgage will help you buy a property, so for a mortgage to offer better value, there must be other benefits; otherwise you may as well just buy the cheapest one, right?

Now before we go any further, I need to head off the sillier critics who spend their time lobbing rocks at people who do them out of a profit by telling the truth. For the record, loud and clear, I do not believe that the cheapest loan is the best. Far from it.

Having said that, I do believe that once you have a list of loans that meet your needs the cheapest from THAT list is the best one for you. The rest either come with stuff that you DON'T need and charge you more for it or cost you more even though you are getting essentially the same thing. From were I sit, taking the cheapest deal that works for you and using any savings to get mortgage free faster beats fattening the merchant's bottom line every time.

If the price is right

I don't know if you ever watched The Price is Right, but it was (and in some countries, still is) a game show based on contestants guessing the right price for different goods. The contestant who guesses closest to the retail value of the goods, without going over the price, wins those goods. In line with the traditional game show formula, contestants were randomly drawn from the studio audience to participate.

The show works because the contestants are everyday people who understand that a dollar is a dollar, even though some may work harder for their dollar than others. For the most part, contestants can ballpark their guess reasonably well as they are likely to have spent money on a similar item or seen it advertised somewhere at a certain price. This is true for most things we buy.

Of course the show's producers pick and choose products to make it deliberately challenging for participants, just like the merchants pick and choose the information they tell you and the costs they use to calculate their promotional interest rates.

To win, contestants needed to guess the price of common goods which they then won as prizes, if the price was near enough.

When it comes to the cost of a mortgage, most people don't have a clue. In fact I have never met a person who doesn't work in the finance industry that has come within cooee of estimating the likely cost of their mortgage. By cooee, I mean that most people underestimate it by 50% or more. So when it comes to the most significant financial decision of their lives, for many, the price is... well... who knows?

Without a reliable method for comparing the price of different mortgage options, how on earth do you know whether you are paying too much, whether paying an extra $5 a month will get you exactly what you need, or whether you are actually getting a bargain?

The frighteningly simple answer is that you don't. But you should and you can.

Taking out the Garbage

The Total Individual Cost (TIC) is the projected cost of your mortgage based on your individual situation. That is:

- ✓ Your Equity/Deposit
- ✓ Your Loan Amount
- ✓ Your Loan Term
- ✓ Your Security Property
- ✓ Your Required Functions and Features

It is based on minimum repayments and is reported to you in dollars and cents.

What makes TIC different to any other comparison standard is that it fixes GIGO by increasing the relevance, quantity and quality of information that goes in to the formula. In other words, it changes the 'G's in GIGO from 'Garbage' to 'Good Stuff' then gives you a cost in every day, understandable terms.

TIC has not been widely implemented in Australia because the merchants claim it adds too much cost, which is of course, bollox. But then, who wants the fox looking after the hen house anyway (think "The Six o'clock Swill").

The real reason merchants hate it is that a TIC eliminates wriggle room. It makes merchants accountable and leaves them exposed to do battle on the thing you want to drive as hard as you possibly can…

Price.

The use of TIC is not widespread amongst merchants needing subterfuge in order to sell their loans. However sophisticated investors, researchers, commercial borrowers, and borrowers agents have been calculating and relying on TIC for years.

Of course merchants and their smoke blowers may try to convince you that TIC is the same as a comparison rate, however it isn't.

TIC works, Advertised Comparison Rates don't.

There are five crucial differences between common measures like Advertised Comparison Rates and TIC.

1. TIC includes all fees required to establish; maintain then close your mortgage. It includes charges that can only be calculated when your individual situation is known (i.e. Lender's Mortgage Insurance) and also includes non-lender charges you might be asked to pay such as brokerage.

2. TIC includes interest rate discounts and savings.

3. TIC is based on YOUR loan term and YOUR loan amount.

4. TIC can be used effectively for <u>any</u> loan with <u>any</u> mix of products, including all interest only products.

5. TIC is a dollars and cents result, so you always know how much extra you are paying or how much you are saving.

TIC can also support you in making decisions within the loan itself. For example, how much do you save or spend by changing your loan term; your loan amount; or paying interest only for the first year or the first few years?

But that's not the end of it either. Unlike Advertised Comparison Rates, TIC helps you when it comes to refinancing decisions. By comparing the remaining TIC of your current loan, with new loans enthusiastically pitched at you by all too clever sales people, you will get an objective view on the cost and benefit of making a switch. You'd be surprised how often merchants will claim a saving that doesn't really exist.

The shocking cost differences you have discovered with me throughout Mortgage Free, Debt Free have all been revealed to you using TIC.

Let's take a look at an example relying on Advertised Comparison Rates of two real life loans that were quoted by the lenders late January 2010[1]. Both are similar products however what we really need to focus on is that the Advertised Comparison Rates makes the price appear quite similar as well.

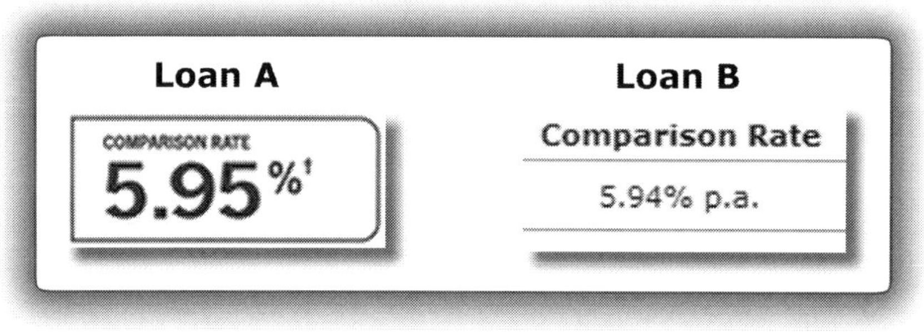

These are Advertised Comparison Rates for mortgages that have the same basic features. Which is cheaper and by how much?

It is only by calculating the TIC for each loan that we can understand the real price difference. Let's say you want to borrow $350,000 for a property you are purchasing for $398,000. You plan to take a loan term of 25 years and you have come to a shortlist of just two loans. Loan A and Loan B.

Despite the seemingly small difference in the Advertised Comparison Rate, the difference in Total Individual Cost is stark.

---

[1] By the time I finalised this book for publication in January 2011 (just one year down the track), the interest rates on both of these products, and the average new mortgage amount had all increased. Although I updated the other examples in this book with the new rates and loan amounts, I decided to leave this example as is. You will understand why by the time you finish reading "There's no such thing as perfect" in just a few pages.

Loan A has a TIC of $334,807. That is, based on current interest rates, fee waivers and by making minimum monthly repayments, you would fork out almost $335,000 in interest and fees. Although this comparison was done when interest rates were very, VERY low, you would still spend almost as much in interest and fees as you borrowed in the first place. Don't forget, you also have to repay the $350,000 as well.

For an ordinary borrower, *Loan B* has a TIC of $330,134, which is a saving of almost $5,000 on *Loan A*. Although that's a worthwhile saving, it also assumes you still made the mistake of "Paying retail" for both loans. This far into Mortgage Free, Debt Free and you are not just smarter, but also more informed than an ordinary borrower. You know that there are further savings to be had and they are easy to get.

In fact when you compare each TIC you quickly realise that *Loan B* actually delivers a saving of more than $30,000 simply by turning on The Free Money Strategy. Of course you get mortgage free much faster as well.

Imagine learning this after you took out *Loan A*. Ouch[1].

I know that for most of Mortgage Free, Debt Free I have been trash talking the use of rates to choose your loan and I still think it is a bad idea.

However if you are a die-hard, "the old way is the best way" or "small numbers are easier" reader, then make sure you always use a Personal Comparison Rate.

Never use an Advertised Comparison Rate.

You must also make sure that your Personal Comparison Rate is calculated on cash flows from the TIC. Otherwise you are probably better off simply tossing a coin. Heads Loan A, Tails Loan B.

---

[1] See the footnote on the opposite page. The news gets even worse.

TIC it or flick it

Picture this. You have bought a house knowing that it needs to be painted before you move in and you don't have time to do it yourself. You crack the yellow pages and let your fingers do the walking, calling the first painter whose ad appeals to you.

After a brief introduction, the voice at the other end of the phone tells you that a standard three bedroom house costs $1500 plus paint plus sanding. It will also be more expensive if the house is bigger than the standard house, they add.

"Mine's pretty average, but it has four bedrooms, not three. How much would that cost?" you ask.

"It's complicated," the voice replies. "You have to factor in usage rates and paint density. Humidity can also play into it, as well as the porosity of the walls…"

"Sure, but I really would like to know how much it will cost me. If I measure up, will you give me a quote?" you ask.

"We don't work that way, we just bill you as we go."

Unless you have rocks in your head, you would politely hang up the phone; make a cup of tea whilst the absurdity drains from your brain, then pick up the phone again to call a different painter.

My point is that most rational, thinking people wouldn't sign up to spending an unknown amount of money for something as minor as getting their house painted. How smart is it then to choose something as financially crucial as your mortgage without understanding just how expensive or cheap it is compared to others?

The obvious thing to do is get a quote ensuring the basis for quoting is standard across all loans, lenders and options. What?

Don't worry, it sounds complicated, but it's not. With the right tools and some honest help, you can get quotes in a few steps if you opt to DIY or one step if you use a fair dinkum mortgage broker, or a borrowers agent. Now before we zip ahead with the how-to, there's something really important to remember.

There's no such thing as perfect

In life, nothing is perfect, but that doesn't stop things from getting as close to perfection as possible. It pays to remember there is always a margin for error, a chance that you will come up short.

Standard TIC calculations use minimum monthly repayments, based on today's interest rates because they are the current certainties. However another certainty is that interest rates will change and you will also make extra payments (hopefully).

A TIC is a forecast indication, not a definite real life cost. When a TIC is calculated, it 'freezes' certain variables such as interest rates, that will vary over time. Change those variables and you change your TIC. As interest rates rise, the total individual cost you pay in real life becomes higher than the TIC indicated back when you were making comparisons. Conversely if rates fall or you pay above minimum, the lower your real life costs will be.

However unlike an Advertised Comparison Rate where for many reasons the loan with the lowest rate could easily be the most expensive, TIC is extremely reliable. There is only one way you will end up paying more for a mortgage with the lowest TIC - you cop a penalty. Remember "Missing the catch"? You must always make sure that you are aware of and understand potential catches laid by your friendly merchants before you sign anything. While you're just a page or two away from learning the simple way to do exactly that, there are important concepts you must first understand. Now stay with me for a moment, because this is important.

There are two types of costs you will pay for any mortgage – recurring costs and once off costs.

Recurring costs are charges that appear day after day, month after month. They continue to grow the longer you have your loan. For the most part these charges are interest on the money you owe and ongoing maintenance costs, such as monthly or annual fees. Recurring costs, as a proportion of your TIC, are less affected by loan term because they are linked to the duration of your loan. For example, if you have your loan for one year you pay just one year's worth of interest and maintenance costs; keep your mortgage for two years and you are up for two years worth of interest and so on.

"Once off" costs are an entirely different story. These costs are the many different fees and charges you pay to open and close your loan. They do not grow over time and are the "spent money" that borrowers often forget or miss until it's too late. Once off costs can amount to tens of thousands of dollars and include fees like those nasty early payment penalties, LMI and legal disbursements. It should be no surprise that the biggest charges belonging to the "once off" family cannot be found in Advertised Comparison Rates. Once off costs will often keep you locked into a poorly performing loan or lender. Leave the lender in one year and you write off a big lump of money. Leave after two years and you still write off that same big lump of money. The longer you stay with your lender, the less significant this write off will be when compared to the overall cost of your loan. However leave early and the impact can be huge.

A Risk Profile helps you account for the impact of once off costs. It does not include ordinary recurring charges such as interest, or maintenance fees. However it does include fees like:

- Application Fees
- Valuation Fees
- Facility Establishment Fees
- Legal and Settlement Fees
- Rate Lock Fees
- LMI, REF or similar Fees
- Early payout penalties Fees
- Discharge Fees

Risk Profiles forecast the cost of getting out of your mortgage if things change and you need to boogie. For example, a moment ago in "Taking out the Garbage" we looked at two similar variable rate loans, which I called *Loan A* and *Loan B*. Using the same scenario, the risk profiles chart like this:

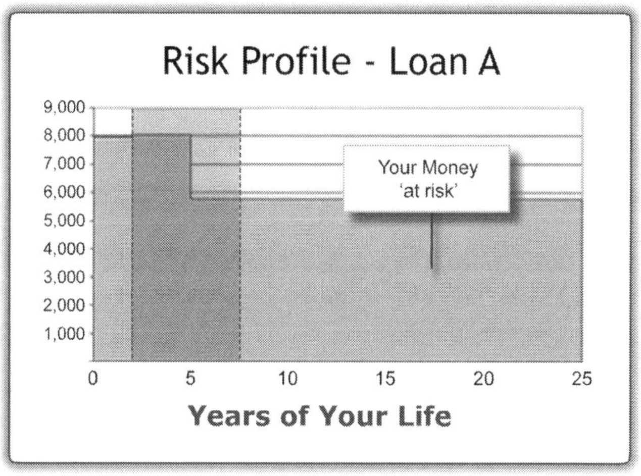

The Risk Profile for Loan A. The shaded area between the dotted vertical lines marks approximately 2-7 years which according to Fujitsu are high risk times.

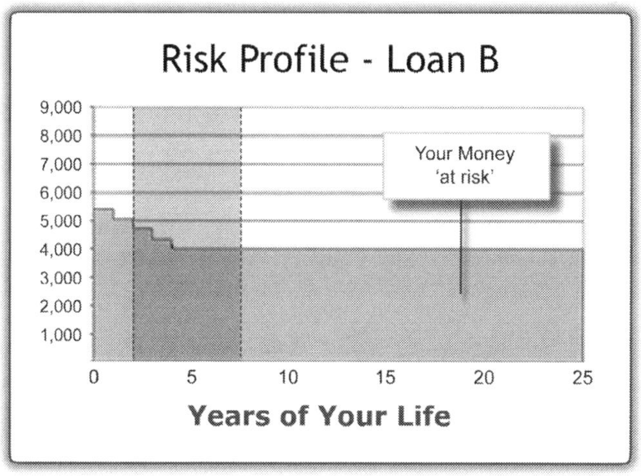

The Risk Profile for Loan B for the identical borrower.

Looking at these charts, you should be able to see the Risk for *Loan A* <u>is higher and stays higher</u> for longer than it does for *Loan B*.

In other words, you are more locked into *Loan A*. However that might be a risk you are prepared to take if *Loan A* is significantly better value than *Loan B*.

Of course you might remember that although the Comparison Rates for these loans differed by bugger all, the TIC for *Loan A* is over $30,000 more expensive than *Loan B*.

Put simply *Loan A* costs more and has more risk too.

Proof of the pudding:

Both *Loan A* and *Loan B* are real life loans. All figures used were as quoted by the lenders in January 2010.

Back then, the latest Canstar CANNEX Home Loan Star Ratings Report, declared *Loan A* "Outstanding Value", awarding it 5 stars.

Canstar CANNEX rated *Loan B* inferior, awarding it 4 Stars.

Whether either of these loans should get any stars is a moot point, however using TIC and Risk Profiles, the smart money says these rankings were back to front.

Blast forward just one year to January 2011 when it was time to finalise the book for publication and things have really changed.

Loan A didn't just lock you in harder than *Loan B,* the interest rates on *Loan A* were jacked up harder in the meantime as well. A lot harder. The TIC on *Loan A* is now almost $60,000 more than *Loan B* on the Free Money Strategy. Ouch.

In less than a year, Canstar CANNEX dropped their star rating on *Loan A* from 5 stars to 3 stars.

While Canstar CANNEX can cut and run on their rating faster than you could say "woops – did I say that", if you relied on their ratings at all, you would be trapped into an outrageously expensive loan for years to come.

Just the facts ma'am

If you are the least bit normal you are probably feeling a little overwhelmed with the math and detail required to get your decision right. Thoughts like, "That sounds great, but how do I do it?" are probably starting to bubble to the surface.

Without doubt the easiest and most intelligent way to get your loan right is to track down a good borrowers agent and use them. These professionals understand the importance of TIC, risks, the pros and the cons and your agent works exclusively for you. However, I also understand that using an agent has you reaching into your pocket when you might not want to - even though I still think you should.

Despite disagreeing with a decision to go it alone, I can't leave you stuck out there unarmed and at the mercy of clever merchants. So I spent a great deal of time and money to give you the tool that delivers only what you need to make proper comparisons. No smoke, no mirrors and no clever sales tricks. The math is done for you including TIC and Risk Profiles. All you need to do is compare the results.

In less time than it will probably take you to read "Just the facts ma'am" you will be able to pick a winner out of two or three different options using the most reliable and relevant information in the market place today.

It's called a KeyFacts Quote Maker and it is absolutely free for anybody to use. You, mortgage brokers, borrowers agents and lenders alike.

The KeyFacts Quote Maker produces standard credit quotes based on your individual situation, allowing you to easily compare value between **any** mortgage broker, bank, building society, credit union and non-bank lender.

So let's look at the facts.

Red light, yellow light

On your journey here, you learned that getting the right features in your loan is the most important step. After all a cheap anything that doesn't work isn't a bargain, it's a con.

You also learned that the same feature name with one lender may mean something quite different when talking with a different merchant. Remember "It's life Jim, but not as we know it"? If this happens on a feature you need you could have a real problem.

All credit quotes generated using the KeyFacts Quote Maker use a traffic light system on each important feature we have discussed in this book. Green means that the loan has the feature and it is top of the line; Amber shows there is a catch such as a fee or limitation, so if you really want this feature you should look a little closer at the merchants fine print; and Red means stop, the loan doesn't have that feature.

Simple huh?

It works because the Quote Maker asks the questions using the right industry jargon and limits the responses a merchant can enter. This removes the wriggle room. These answers are then run through an algorithm to produce the traffic light ranking for each feature.

Total Individual Cost

Each credit quote includes a series of TIC calculations. The summary is estimated assuming the full term of the loan; however you can also see a TIC on a year by year basis.

This gives you the opportunity to quickly see the risk profile at any point throughout the life of the loan should you decide to or need to leave it early. Annual summaries make it simple to see the impact of establishment fees and penalties that the merchants ordinarily avoid mentioning until well after you have applied for your loan. Before you even begin the sign up process you will see just how locked in you become at any point in time if you buy that loan.

Personal Comparison Rates

You already know that I am dead against using rates as a basis for comparison as most of us don't work for, eat or use percentages anywhere else. Just the same, each credit quote also lists a Personal Comparison Rate alongside each TIC. This means you can easily see the Personal Comparison Rate if you close your mortgage at the end of the first year, fifth year or any other year for that matter.

The only time you might not be able to see a Personal Comparison Rate is when one or more of your loans has an evergreen interest-only facility (Interest-only for the full term).

On the bright side, a TIC makes more sense anyway and you will always be able to see that.

The main fees

To help you understand where you are spending your money, you can see a breakdown of the main fees used to calculate your TIC. These fees are already factored into your Total Individual Cost so you don't have to worry about doing any extra math. However they are included to help you or your borrower's agent easily verify the reliability of your merchant's quote when your loan documents arrive. I'll explain how to do that shortly. The main fees include:

1. Application Fees
2. Valuation Fees
3. Facility Establishment Fees
4. Legal and Settlement Fees
5. Rate Lock Fees
6. LMI, REF or similar Fees
7. Early payout penalties Fees
8. Discharge Fees

Of course these aren't all the fees you might be charged, but they are quotes on the fees you will definitely be charged but don't normally find out about until it's too late.

Other fees such as late payment fees, over limit interest rates and similar are not included in your TIC. These fees are excluded as they are avoidable by simply managing your loan well. Nonetheless, you will still see these exception based charges in your loan contracts if you want to understand these fees as well.

Commissions (If a broker provides the quote)

Commissions are disclosed in dollars and cents so you can easily see what the lender is paying for introducing your loan. Remember though, if you go to the lender directly, they keep that commission as profit anyway.

Raising the standard

As we talked about in "Swallowing the standard", the term 'standard' means "a measure serving as a basis by which others can be compared".

What you have just read about is a credit quote produced to the KeyFacts Standard. It will not apply to credit quotes generated by other means, so it pays to look out for the KeyFacts mark.

It looks like this:

Any quote bearing the KeyFacts mark has been developed strictly adhering to seven important ethical standards:

1. The consumer needs are the most important of all.

2. Results must be comprehensive and personalised to the individual consumer situation.

3. Facts affecting the core usability of any loan or service must be accessible, understandable and comparable for the consumer.

4. Costs to establish, maintain and close a loan or service must be clearly available, understandable and simple for the consumer to compare.

5. Calculations must follow industry standard formulas where they exist and be available for independent audit.

6. Formulas and calculation methods must be identical across all similar tools for any lender, any loan, any loan amount or any service.

7. A version of each tool must be publicly accessible; use identical formulas and calculation methods to all similar tools endorsed with the KeyFacts mark; and be free for anyone to use as often as they like, whenever they like for whatever loan, lender or service they like.

These seven ethical standards are critical to ensure that each quote honestly represents the key areas that affect your financial outcome as a borrower. Skip just one of those ethical standards and your results become, well, less ethical.

Pop back to "Taking out the Garbage" where we learned that a loan with an Advertised Comparison Rate just 0.01% higher than a competitors, cost over $30,000 more when borrowing $350,000. That's because Advertised Comparison Rates do not comply with any of the 7 principles that define the KeyFacts Standard. Most 'in-house' mortgage broker software would struggle to meet just two.

Are you worth 5 minutes?

I think you are and then some. You should too.

It takes merchants and borrowers agents less than 5 minutes to produce a credit quote for you using the KeyFacts Quote Maker.

Any good borrowers agent will provide credit quotes to you without the need to ask. The simplicity and reliability offered by quotes meeting the KeyFacts Standard helps the agent work with you to easily compare and identify the right solution.

However if you are dealing directly with a merchant, you may need to insist that you require a credit quote before you will make an application. Merchants that genuinely believe in transparency will happily oblige, however others might put up a little resistance.

One reason merchants refuse to quote to the KeyFacts Standard is as simple as they don't think you are worth 5 minutes of their time. Fair enough, they've got profits to make and products to sell; but why should you sign with them for the next 10, 20 or 30 years when they are already too busy for you?

The only other reason is the merchant is concerned that their product will not appear quite so appealing to you when the smoke and mirrors are stripped away.

If your merchant says they don't already have the KeyFacts Quote Maker, send them to the KeyFacts website where they can download it and use it for free.

If you find that you have to ask for a quote, make sure you give them a realistic timeframe to send it to you. Then sit back and wait.

As a rule of thumb, I allow two working days for a merchant to give me the answers. This follows some very basic principles.

- It's a mortgage, not open heart surgery. You're not going to die if you don't get the answers immediately. Two days is enough time to get the right answers from the departments that really know rather than getting fast, but wrong answers from sales people who don't.

- If they can't give you a simple quote within two working days, then they are light on the ground with skill and resources. Quoting is part of selling. Selling is the core function of all merchants. If they can't give you such a basic service whilst they're in sales mode, what hope do you have once you are locked into a mortgage?

If you don't hear back from the lender within your required time frame, you can't see the TIC so give them the flick.

Either they've got something to hide or their poor quality of service is on display for you to see. Quite frankly, you deserve better, no matter what their excuse.

Get quotes BEFORE you make an application. Sure, the merchants and people who don't know any better will tell you that you are not stitched up until you sign the loan contracts.

However by the time you're looking at those it's already too late. You just won't have time to start looking all over again.

An Insurance Policy

Like all calculations, the KeyFacts Quote Maker has a risk of Garbage In Garbage Out. As we have already learned, this garbage has the potential to cost you money, when it shouldn't.

However unlike Advertised Comparison Rates and the stuff your merchant provides, you can easily spot the garbage, and then do something about it if you have a quote. You can see it, because like your loan contracts, your quote breaks the fees out item by item. You can do something about it because the fee was quoted to you when the merchant knew your individual situation. The wriggle room all but disappears.

When your loan contracts arrive

Your loan contracts are the be all and end all of your loan agreement. In amongst them, you will find a table of fees and charges the lender requires you to pay to set up; maintain and exit your loan.

> If you have a borrowers agent, they may do these steps for you.

Simply check those fees against the main fees quoted to you by the merchant. If fees have increased or been added since your quote, send the credit quote and the fees page of the contracts to your merchant or agent telling them to update your loan agreements to match the quote or reimburse you for the difference. Be polite and set a time frame for them to respond.

Reasonable Reasons

You may see differences in the interest rate which is always going to happen over time so this in itself is reasonable.

However increased fees between a quote and loan contracts are a no-no. That said, it does not stop merchants from changing or adding fees, it just makes you more aware that they have done it. Still, it is important to understand there may be a reasonable reason a fee has changed.

The main one I can think of involves mortgage insurance. LMI charges are calculated using (a) the amount you are borrowing and (b) the value of your property. Differences to either the loan amount or property valuation will usually vary the premium. If your property valuation comes in lower than expected, or you increase the amount you want to borrow, your mortgage insurance premium will go up.

The only other reasonable reason I can think of is that you are looking at an old quote. Old usually means more than two months and in that time, fees can definitely change.

Other than that, I don't think there is any reasonable reason to consider, however what's reasonable is really up to you. If you hear a new reasonable reason or would like to check if I think a reason is reasonable, please email me at michael.lee@keyfacts.com.au so I can work it through and share the knowledge.

Dealing with indifference

If you can't get a reasonable reason from your merchant and they refuse to fix the loan contracts or reimburse you, then you should make a formal, written complaint to the merchant outlining the options you are considering taking.

Like all quotes, how strictly you want to enforce it is up to you. Some people will fight to the ends of the earth purely for principle; others couldn't be bothered chasing $500, even though they should. The most common options available are:

1. A written complaint to ASIC – Whether you are dealing with a Lender, Mortgage Broker or borrowers agent, they are all licensed by ASIC (www.asic.gov.au).

   Taking this action works because legitimate complaints jeopardise the licence of the merchant which is required for them to advise on or sell credit.

2. Posting your complaint to consumer websites such as Not Good Enough (www.notgoodenough.org).

   Taking this action works because it adds to the honest dialogue about your service provider and could warn off other consumers from experiencing the same problem.

3. A written complaint to the Ombudsman. This could be the Financial Ombudsman Service (www.fos.org.au) or the Credit Ombudsman Service. (www.cosl.com.au). No matter who you are dealing with, they may belong to one, the other or both ombudsman services.

Taking this action should work as the Ombudsman service arbitrates disputes between members and consumers.

4. A written complaint to their professional body. Lenders may belong to MFAA; Brokers may belong to FBAA or MFAA or even both. Borrower's agents are for now, likely to belong to MFAA until such time as a professional association for borrower's agents is established.

   This action may work if they have a current membership as it might alarm the merchant or agent and prompt them into positive action. However these associations tend to be more focussed on the interests of their members rather your interests as a borrower. For the most part, the MFAA and FBAA are powerless to deal with merchants or agents that do not have current membership at the time of your complaint.

If you need any of these businesses, visit their website to get further information and in the case of Associations and Ombudsman services, to check if your merchant is a member. Most complaints can be lodged online to simplify and accelerate the process.

Whether you still go ahead with signing your loan contracts is up to you. In many cases you may have to, however before you do, get your formal demand off to the merchant to help you seek reimbursement later on. It is worthwhile copying the Professional Indemnity Insurer if you have their details as well.

How to choose a mortgage broker

WHAT? Didn't see that one coming? Well, no matter what path you choose, I respect it and want to make sure you have as much useful information as possible. I figured that once you close this book for the final time this year, you will either:

- Use a borrower's agent to do everything now that you have a much better idea of exactly what "everything" is.

- Do most of it yourself and get some professional help as required verifying things like TIC and Risk Profiles.

- Hire a mortgage broker using a Pro-Consumer Agreement.

- Do all of it yourself without outside help and without getting proper quotes. With all due respect, this is a little nuts.

- Turn to a lender or ordinary mortgage broker for advice. It's your money, spend it how you will.

No matter which of these paths you take, the reality is that a good mortgage broker will save you something providing they can deliver the right loan.

In the very least, they will save time in arranging your loan by collating the documentation and following up the lender on your behalf. They can also save you money by using their buying power to obtain better discounts from lenders as well as significantly reducing your loan costs with cashback deals.

Also important is that you establish a history and rapport with a person that you can easily call to talk through changes to your mortgage or your circumstances. Then, when it's time to move you don't have to start explaining yourself to a stranger that doesn't know you or your situation.

The basic rules for choosing a mortgage broker are simple.

1. Stay alert and cynical.

2. Never deal with a broker that will not provide you with a credit quote meeting the KeyFacts Standard. It takes them less than 5 minutes and other than that, it's free.

3. Identify any lenders you are particularly interested in before you talk with a broker.

4. Ensure all lenders that you may be interested in appear in the broker's lender panel. A wider range can offer better flexibility if your needs change further down the track.

5. Get confirmation that the broker can deal with all of the lenders on their panel that interest you. Remember, brokers can advertise a large lender panel yet only be authorised to deal with one or two of them.

6. Ask for a copy of your broker's professional indemnity insurance certificate of currency. Check that it is current, that your broker is insured and you are happy with the limit of indemnity (sometimes called the sum insured).

7. Check ASIC's website to ensure the broker is licensed and does not have any reported history of poor behaviour.

8. Get your broker to complete a KeyFacts Standard Credit Quote for his or her top three recommendations before you sign. I know I have mentioned this before, but it is really important!

9. Wait at least 24 hours after hearing your brokers' recommendations before signing an application. This gives you time to make sure you have thought of all of your questions and they have been answered properly.

10. Check for your broker's independence.

Most of the rules for choosing a mortgage broker are pretty straight forward. However, some of you may think I have lost the plot because I've mentioned independence after giving the idea such a hard time earlier on. Bear with me. This is about <u>arranging</u> your mortgage not getting advice. Taking advice from any broker is risky regardless of whether they are independent or not, although using a Pro-Consumer Agreement removes a big chunk of that risk.

Choosing the right broker can improve your chances of getting a better quality of service, a more personal approach and a better price. The more independent your broker is, the more able they are to offer you these three distinct advantages.

Brokers have better buying power and negotiation experience than you do as an individual which can often result in a better retail rate. Then of course there is the "The Free Money Strategy". In combination, these two factors offer unparalleled savings. While price is not everything, it ranks at the top of the list if you plan to get mortgage free faster and are getting the identical loan. Not similar. Identical.

By using a broker you also establish a history and ongoing relationship with the person who acts as your broker. They can move with you as your needs change.

Finally, if there is any funny business from the lender or your broker for that matter, your broker is directly on the hook, at least to some extent anyway.

The alternative to an independent mortgage broker is one that belongs to a franchise. If you're not sure what a franchise is, think McDonalds, which is why I call franchised brokers 'McBrokers'. A McBroker is any broker who is tied to a big, sometimes well known brand. Let's call them The Big Brand.

Without doubt, McDonalds is a respectable restaurant delivering a popular balance between value, convenience and taste. However that doesn't mean the kid flipping burgers could get you a better price on mince. It also doesn't mean he could whip off his uniform and zip around to your place to cook the best spaghetti bolognaise you've ever eaten.

McBrokers generally benefit from reflected glory. This is where you think of your McBroker as having the experience and robustness of The Big Brand, yet you may wind up in the hands of a very small business which was only recently established and has purchased rights to promote itself as The Big Brand.

McBrokers also tend to be a popular training ground for newcomers, who, once they become skilled, start up an independent brokerage. If your McBroker moves on to become independent, your real history and personal relationship leaves with them.

The problem with this is that McBrokers are usually subjected to contracts that prevent them from helping you once they leave The Big Brand. Even though your ex-McBroker still brokers and they're more experienced than when you first dealt with them, even though they still remember you and you them, The Big Brand usually stops you from dealing with them. Sure you can probably start all over again with a new McBroker but to them and The Big Brand, you are just a file on a computer somewhere. If the new McBroker moves on as many do, well I guess you can always start again, again.

Regardless of whether you use a McBroker or an independent mortgage broker, misjudging the experience and capability of either can be expensive in both time and money so make sure you or your borrower's agent checks them out thoroughly.

The final risk when dealing with McBrokers is they must toe the corporate line. This means that somebody at the big end of town and hungry for profits decides which mortgages McBrokers sell and how they sell them.

With more fingers in the pie, McBrokers must sell more and earn The Big Brand big profits from larger commissions. So with a McBroker you often get less choice than you will with an independent. This limited, commission-driven range is then served to you using a cleverly refined sales process and impressive in-house software all designed to help you say 'yes'.

That's 'yes' to paying an extra $30,000, $40,000 or more on that loan with a McBroker doing it their way, than if you had a Pro-Consumer Agreement or hired a borrower's agent. Do it your way not theirs.

Revision: Turning the tables

And there you have it. The different ways that you can go shopping including the way that it's always been done and the ways that it should be done.

You should now understand that:

- ✓ The only way to get a professional adviser is to hire one.
- ✓ You can remove most of the commission bias from brokers by using Pro-Consumer Agreement.
- ✓ TICs work and comparison rates don't.
- ✓ Standardised quotes make comparison easy.
- ✓ Lenders, brokers and borrowers agents can use the KeyFacts Quote Maker for free.
- ✓ It takes less than 5 minutes to prepare an honest, fully transparent credit quote using the Quote Maker.
- ✓ Quotes help you compare and hold your merchant or agent to account.
- ✓ The differences between an Independent Mortgage Broker and a McBroker are important.

Well, you're ready. The only thing left is to go shopping for yourself, choose the loan that fits you and is the easiest one for you to eliminate.

Once you've got it, your next goal is to get rid of it.

STEP 5

Get rid of it

"Knowing is not enough; we must apply. Willing is not enough; we must do."
Johann Wolfgang von Goethe (1749 – 1832)

No matter which way you look at it, being debt free, or at least having as little debt as possible gives you more freedom and financial stability. This is not an argument against making investments or even using credit as a vehicle to purchase them.

However if you were to choose between two otherwise identical investments, one without debt and one with, only a fool would choose the latter.

So, now that you've got the most effective debt you could arrange, let's get rid of it.

P.S. If you have a bookmark, put it here before you retire Mortgage Free, Debt Free to the bookshelf. This is the section you will need to come back to in a few years time.

P.P.S. Just in case it's not common sense, if your father, mother, brother, sister, partner, friend could use this book, buy them their own copy. You'll need to keep coming back to this one to help you stay ahead of the game.

Stick to your strategy

It's a little simplistic isn't it? But, once you've set your mortgage up the right way, that's the answer.

If you took your loan with a lender you can get through a mortgage broker, you should already have The Free Money Strategy ticking away in the background. However if you really want to nail your debt as quickly as possible, you still have to do some heavy lifting. Add these rules to the things you must do to beat the banks and the brokers:

1. Avoid all new, non-investment debt including personal loans, interest free offers and rolling balance credit cards. Save for what you want using the "The Savings Plan" strategy.

2. Redraw only the amount you have deposited toward a savings goal once you have reached that goal and avoid all other redraws.

3. Increase your repayments whenever you can.

4. Never reduce repayments.

5. Monitor your progress honestly and take action to get back on track when you need to.

Oh, of course there is that other thing… Don't ever set and forget.

Set and forget = Set and regret

If you've ticked all the boxes along the way, you should now have either the most effective or one of the most effective loans for your needs. Your repayments are set up and split out according to your strategy, your banking is sorted. Life once more slips into its steady rhythm.

For the most part, things will take care of themselves, although you should continue to watch your spending and check your statements for surprise charges, rate hikes or general errors. Look into getting statements sent monthly and check them when they arrive. Shorter statements are easier to check. Once again, there are a thousand and one self-help books with tips for staying on top of your spending and your money. Buy a good one, read it and make sure you try the ideas out.

In the meantime, know that lenders are like car makers. The one that's on top today may be a ways down the list next year or the year after that. Even if your needs don't change and your strategies are working tickety boo, you should check what's out there from time to time and make sure your lender is still toward the top of the pack, if not AT the top of the pack.

If you've taken a fixed rate, you should always work out whether you want to re-fix or not about six weeks before your current rate expires. Then regardless of your choice to fix or stay variable, re-shop your loan as soon as you possibly can.

However if you've stayed variable, how often you check the market is up to you. As a rough guide, a casual skim every year or so with a quick rate check on a web site such as www.yourmortgage.com.au should be fine. If your rate has magically slipped toward the middle or worse, the bottom half of the heap, or if your lender comes up short on something that is really important to you, then you should take a look to see what's around.

No matter what, all variable rate borrowers that didn't pay Lenders Mortgage Insurance should take a serious look at refinancing every 3 to 5 years. However if you did pay mortgage insurance, you could probably stretch that to every 5 to 8 years.

As with most things, the more often you do it and the more properly you do it, the better your results will be. This obviously excludes smoking, drinking, taking illicit drugs, adultery and any other life, happiness or health altering thing you want to add to the list.

It is very important to understand that "taking a serious look" is completely different to actually refinancing your loan. The former is keeping your lender honest and not spending any money in the process; the latter is sacking your lender and paying to do it.

If you followed the steps and ticked the boxes you've learned about here, you probably will only ever take a serious look and will never actually need to refinance.

Doing the proper preparation and planning that you have learned about in Mortgage Free, Debt Free before you take your loan, or having a professional do it for you, means you would be plain unlucky to ever need to refinance it. It's not to say that it won't happen, more that it will only happen if your lender turns out to be an utter bastard; new and significant financial needs arise; or life just takes an unexpected turn.

If you already had your mortgage before you picked up this book, you probably will want to refinance it the moment you take your first serious look. But that could easily be the last time that you ever feel the need to do anything other than look.

Taking a serious look at refinancing

Wow, that time sure went fast, didn't it? You've been in your loan for a while and if you followed the steps to design and choose your debt and stuck with your strategy you are already well ahead of the game. But something has tripped your switch to take a serious look at refinancing, so let's learn how to do that well.

If you diligently followed the steps in Mortgage Free, Debt Free the only reason you should really need to do this is to make sure that your lender has held up their end of the bargain and stayed competitive or, something has seriously and unexpectedly changed in your life.

If however, you have just picked up Mortgage Free, Debt Free for the first time and jumped here from the index, then start at the beginning of the book, not here. You've got a lot to catch up on. For everyone else, there are some really important rules to follow when taking a serious look.

Your current loan is your standard

The mortgage you have today is always the benchmark that you must use when considering any new option. You should always work hard to ensure you stay objective and cool headed when assessing your current lender as well. It's all too easy for people to build a negative impression of their lender over an incident of bad service when they called about a cheque clearance or credit card payment. You shouldn't tolerate bad service, but you should be aware that chasing the idea of better service will cost you money and you ought to find out how much before you jump ship. If you are thinking of refinancing ask your lender for:

1. A discount to save your business.
2. A fresh credit quote based on current loan balances, interest rates (or the discounted one if they say yes) and remaining loan term.
3. Your current payout figure including all exit fees and charges.

The fresh credit quote becomes your standard in terms of cost and functionality.

Add another $200 or so to the current payout figure including all exit fees and charges and it becomes the loan amount you should use when asking other lenders for quotes.

If you are thinking of refinancing to a different type of loan or for different features, or with additional borrowings, you should also ask your lender for a credit quote based on your current loan term, but including the changes you want to achieve your goal.

Keep it apple with apple

The most common mistake made by borrowers and often encouraged by merchants is to compare new loans on a completely different basis to the current loan. This can affect your perceived benefit from switching to a new loan and have you throwing good money after bad. The main areas where this occurs are:

1. Loan Term.
2. Repayments.
3. Repayment Type.
4. Loan Amount.

Loan Term: By varying the loan term, payments may appear lower as repaying your debt is spread over a longer period. Always make sure your loan term for new quotes is based on the remaining term of your current loan or that your fresh credit quote from your existing lender is based on the new loan term that you will take with any new lender - Don't accidentally re-amortise! (see page 153).

Repayments: Make sure payments are factored in on either an identical dollar amount (i.e. $X every fortnight) or simply on minimum monthly repayments. Merchants often demonstrate the benefit of offset accounts by showing all of your income going in, but only the minimum being redrawn which can unrealistically reduce the interest and time taken to repay your loan.

Repayment Type: Make sure both loans are compared on either principal and interest repayments or interest only payments (for the identical interest only period).

Loan Amount: The loan amount for any new lender should be the current payout figure of your existing lender including all exit fees and charges plus the establishment costs with the new lender plus an allowance for government charges ($200 per property ought to cover that).

Keeping things apple with apple becomes less important if your current lender cannot help you with what it is that you want to do. For example, you now want to subdivide your property into four lots then build townhouses on it and your current lender will only allow you to subdivide into two lots. The switching cost then becomes a necessary cost to pursue your desires.

Recover your costs

If you are thinking about switching to another lender, you must make sure you can recover your switching costs within a reasonable time. What reasonable means, is up to you.

Cover your bases

Refinancing to a new loan should be given as much thought, if not more, as when you took your first mortgage. Although you already have a loan, finding the right one to switch to should be done very carefully as it always comes at a cost. Each time you want to refinance, you almost certainly should start at the beginning of this book and make sure you are doing the very best you can at every step along the way.

Of course I know how unrealistic that probably is for you, so rather than starting from the beginning, here's a quick reference of the key topics to help you jump to the information that you need.

If you think…

- All you need is advice from a broker or lender, go back to "Clearing the air" because nothing has changed – page 7.
- You're not really getting anywhere, start reading at "Step 1: Avoid common, costly mistakes" to work out where you went wrong – page 57.
- You would like to get debt free faster, increase your repayments then revisit "Step 2: Choose your weapons" – page 97.
- You need to increase your borrowings, go back to "Step 3: Design your debt" – page 119.
- Your lender is a bastard. Everything else seems fine, go to "Step 4: Turning the tables" – page 159.
- You need to consolidate debt, go forward to "Cushioning credit stress " – page 234.

If you cannot recover your switching costs within a reasonable time, the lender that you are switching to may get stale before you ever get ahead.

Although a ‘reasonable time’ is subjective, it should be no longer than half the amount of time you allow between taking serious looks. i.e. 1.5 to 4 years.

Revision: Get rid of it

You've set your strategy and found the best mortgage you can to use it on, now you just need to get on with it.

- ✓ Implement your strategy.
- ✓ Learn how to better mange your money.
- ✓ Get monthly statements and review them when they arrive.
- ✓ Take a serious look at your mortgage rate and fees against the market every 2 to 3 years or 5 to 8 years if you paid Lenders Mortgage Insurance.
- ✓ Use your current loan as the standard that newcomers must beat.
- ✓ Be careful in allocating costs when comparing your current loan to a new option.
- ✓ Do not switch unless you have to or unless you can recover switching costs within a reasonable time.

Part III: Money Savers, Money Wasters

As I sat down to write Mortgage Free, Debt Free, I decided I would write it based on the Pareto principle. You might also know this as the 80-20 rule which is a useful approximation that suggests 80% of readers can get what they need to know simply by reading and acting on the earlier parts of the book. I did this to save you wading through piles of information that you may only need in some circumstances.

Then again, the more you know, the better your outcome will be. So if you are among the 80% who thinks that you have already discovered what you need to know, you probably could close the book right now and get to it. Probably…

But then you really should read on because you don't know what you don't know and this section could contain an ah-ha moment that saves your bacon.

For the other 20%, you simply MUST read this section whether you want to or not. Sorry.

Lenders Mortgage Insurance (LMI)

Lenders Mortgage Insurance is often misunderstood by borrowers. If you think you might be charged Lenders Mortgage Insurance, then you should definitely read this section. If you don't think you will be subject to Lenders Mortgage Insurance, it's still worth reading the first page at least.

Lenders Mortgage Insurance; Reduced Equity Fee; Loan Equalisation Fee; Mortgage Insurance and LMI. They are all the same thing, but let's call it LMI for the sake of keeping it simple.

When you arrange a mortgage, your lender may 'ask' you to pay LMI. Most people understand that when a lender holds out their hand for money, it must be paid or they simply don't get the loan. But there's a lot more to LMI than that.

Each lender has individual rules on when they will insist you pay LMI. They are not required to advertise their policy and they do not include LMI in Advertised Comparison Rates. While some lenders only charge LMI when you borrow more than 80% of the value of your property, others may charge LMI on every loan.

If you don't get a credit quote before you make an application, merchants probably won't tell you whether LMI applies to your loan or how much it will be other than burying it in your loan contracts. As we know, by the time you're reading those, it's often too late. But that's not the end of the story and definitely not all you need to know about LMI.

You are not protected – at all

The trick to understanding who or what is covered by LMI is to recognise which word to emphasise – it's Lenders Mortgage Insurance. It should really be written "Lender's Mortgage Insurance", however it rarely ever is. LMI is a very expensive insurance policy which may be triggered if your lender forecloses on your property. It protects them against a shortfall between the sale price of the property and the amount you owe to your lender. Your lender takes out this insurance to protect themselves then decides how much of the premium will be paid by you. Although you generally pay the lion's share of that premium, LMI gives you no protection at all.

The bad news does not stop there.

If a mortgage insurer pays out a claim, they are then able to recover that money and associated expenses plus interest, from you.

In everyday terms, it's a lot like paying the insurance premium for a person driving the car in front of you. If you slam into the back of their car the insurance company takes care of them by fixing up the damage. No charge. No fuss.

However even though you paid the premium, you are not insured by the policy and neither is your car. Worse still, the insurance company, which you paid, can and will probably sue you for the cost of the repairs to the other person's car. If you want to be protected, you must take out and pay for another policy as well.

Premium is based on the lender

In the "Taking out the Garbage" case study, the lenders for Loan A and Loan B both required the borrower to pay LMI. One lender quoted a premium a little over $3,500 and the other $5,500. That's almost 60% more on a once off, largely non-refundable fee that does nothing to protect you. Yikes.

Contrary to what merchants tell you, the same scenario arranged with different lenders usually results in different LMI premiums – even if all lenders use the same insurer. There are five factors that influence the premium you will be charged.

The first and most obvious is that one lender may insist that you pay for mortgage insurance while another may not. It comes down to an internal policy.

The second factor is that LMI fees, like premiums on most insurance policies, are risk and exposure based. Exposure relates to the amount of money the insurer may have to pay in the event of a claim. Risk relates to the likelihood that the insurer will have to pay out on a claim.

A major part of that risk, relates to how confident the insurer is in the credit policy and practice of the lender, which of course, is the one that's insured. If the insurer considers one lender to be more risky than the other, they charge a higher premium.

Revisiting our car insurance analogy, think about a Holden Commodore insured with GIO for market value. If a fifty-year-old driver living in the country were to comprehensively insure that car, his premium will almost certainly be a lot cheaper than an eighteen year old male who keeps the Commodore parked on the street in a high-theft, inner-city area. Even though both men are insuring the same car for the same amount with the same cover, it's the driver's statistics that make all the difference to the cost of the premium.

Your mortgage is the Commodore. Your lender is the driver.

> Merchants sticking together - Lenders like St George have been known to pay a cash bonus to brokers for arranging loans requiring LMI.

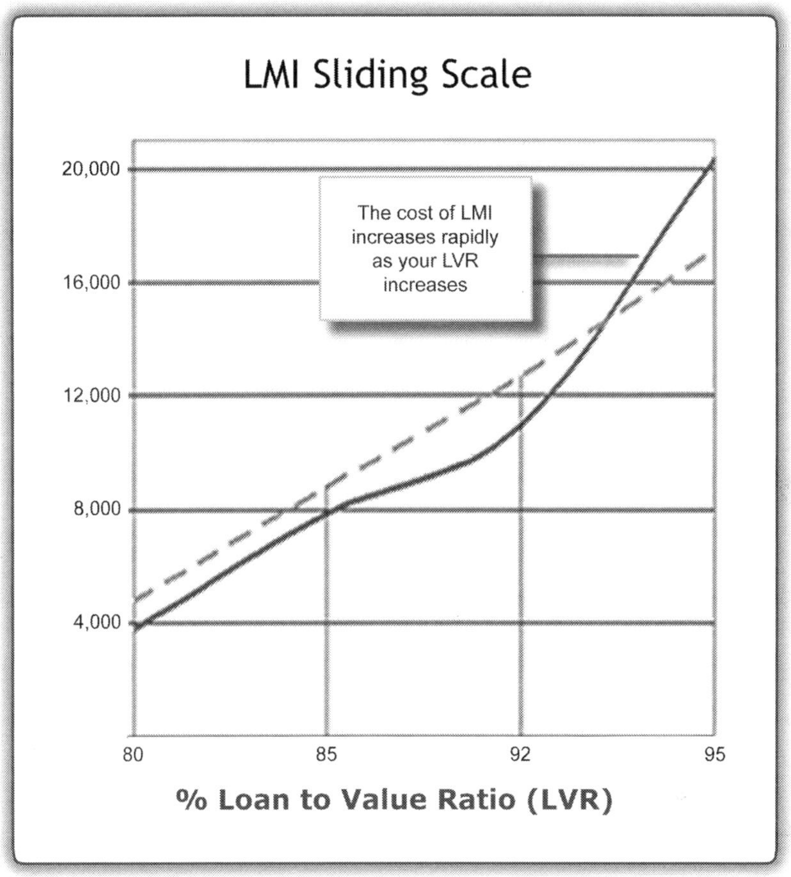

This is a sample LMI premium curve for the same loan amount at common LVR points. Premiums usually rise sharply as LVR increases.

The third factor influencing how much you will pay for LMI is whether the lender subsidises the mortgage insurance premium and to what extent (yes, it actually does happen).

The fourth is the method that a lender adopts to calculate the Loan to Value Ratio (LVR) which is:

$$\text{LVR} = \frac{\text{Amount You Want to Borrow}}{\text{Value of Property/ies}} \times 100$$

If your lender adds the LMI charge to the loan before calculating the actual premium, then you can really jump thresholds as the LVR is beefed up by the extra borrowings for the LMI itself. Although this practice has recently disappeared, never underestimate the chance that it could resurface.

The fifth and final factor influencing the cost of LMI is which insurer your lender uses. Although there are two open access mortgage insurers, a good number of lenders have self-insured options including ANZ, Westpac, St George and ING to name a few.

Although this does not automatically make these lenders or their mortgage insurance options better or cheaper, it can. It also makes anyone who tries to convince you that LMI premiums are ‘pretty much the same’ either a big fat liar or just plain ignorant.

Putting all that aside, LMI can keep you locked into a dud loan, which is just one reason merchants have few qualms about arranging it. The money you pay in LMI is usually a greater cost with a bigger impact on any refinance decision than the commonly complained about Deferred Establishment Fee.

Fortunately both of these ugly fees will show up if you get a good quality credit quote on any loans that interest you. Of course it’s a no-brainer that you should do that BEFORE you make your application.

There are four important things to understand about the real cost of LMI:

1. LMI premiums, like income tax, are calculated on a sliding scale. This scale works increasingly against you if you increase either your Loan Amount or Loan-to-Value Ratio (LVR).

   A small change to either of these variables can result in a massive change in the premium if it steps you into a new threshold.

2. Any estimate a lender gives you over the phone can be wildly different to the premium on your loan contracts.

By insisting on a credit quote that complies with the KeyFacts Standard you have hard evidence which you can use to hold your merchant to account if your loan contracts turn up with a rude shock that wasn't included in the quote.

3. Lenders have different rate scales, meaning that the Loan Amount and LVR thresholds where premiums leap either up or down are different between lenders.

4. Lenders have different abilities to determine when and how much you will pay in LMI.

At the end of the day, LMI is only a part of the Total Individual Cost of your mortgage. Unlike the costs many borrowers focus on, such as interest rate and ongoing fees, LMI is incurred at the beginning of the loan, in a lump sum. You don't just pay LMI; you end up paying interest on it as well!

In instances where you find yourself refinancing within two years, your lender might offer a partial refund and I do mean partial. The maximum refund around at the moment is 40% when a loan is refinanced in the first year. This falls to 20% if your mortgage is paid out in the second year. There is no refund after that and the refund policy varies from lender to lender. Of course.

LMI can be reduced dramatically or avoided completely by:

1. Reducing your Loan to Value Ratio (borrow less, contribute more);

2. Finding lenders that offer LMI concessions for your occupation or LVR;

3. Investigating cross collateralisation or guarantor options.

Do as many of these things as you sensibly can.

Packages (Pro-packs and its mates)

In "Swallowing the standard" we learnt that the Standard Variable Rate is a benchmark rate for each lender, rather than an interest rate anyone actually pays. Pro packs are one important reason for you to ignore any Standard Variable Comparisons. Whether it's called a banking package, professional package or a pro-pack, your rate is discounted a certain percentage off the lender's Standard Variable Rate. To keep it simple, I'll stick with the common vernacular, pro-pack.

The first thing to understand is that a pro-pack is not a loan type. It is an overarching product giving you certain discounts while you continue to pay an ongoing monthly or annual fee. These fees are typically between $300 and $395 per year. Some lenders charge this fee annually; others break it down to a monthly fee. Although this ongoing fee may appear excessive, it is quickly overtaken by the potential interest savings for the right sized loan. This fee also replaces a large suite of other fees, so general banking charges that you might otherwise pay are often reduced or eliminated altogether.

There are also some less promoted benefits, however the most significant, and obvious advantage to most borrowers is a discount off the lender's "Standard Variable Rate".

The size of the discount is generally linked to the size of your overall borrowings and, logically enough, the bigger your debt, the bigger your discount. The rack retail discounts tend to sit between 0.5% and 0.7% p.a. however I have seen and been involved in negotiated discounts as high as 1.0% p.a.

Generally speaking, pro-packs are uneconomical for loans below $250,000. The high monthly or annual fee usually swallows up any saving you get from the puny discount offered for these 'smaller' loans. Even though I struggle to understand the concept, lenders appear to think that a $249,999 mortgage is too small and isn't really worth fighting for.

Go figure....

The actual inclusions and discounts can vary wildly between lenders, so make sure the pro-packs that interest you have discounts and waivers on things that you will use. Generally speaking a Pro-Pack includes:

- ✓ Interest rate discounts on variable rate home loans. Some lenders also discount their fixed rates.
- ✓ Up to four credit cards with no annual fee (this is where the lenders make up the profits from careless borrowers).
- ✓ Free or discounted offset and savings accounts.
- ✓ Discounts on insurances including buildings and landlord protection insurances.
- ✓ Fee waivers on valuations, top ups and switches.

So is a Pro-Pack right for you? It is dangerous to generalise so I won't. The safest way to work it out is to ask a borrower's agent. However assuming you are NOT using a borrower's agent, ask merchants to quote on both a Pro-Pack and their non-Pro-Pack recommendation.

Each lender is likely to have a different Tipping Point at which it becomes sensible for you to either take or reject the packaged option (unless that lender doesn't offer a packaged option). By comparing the quoted TICs for each option you will easily identify where that tipping point is for your situation with each lender.

Fees like Deferred Establishment Fees and Discharge Fees are often charged per loan, not per package.

So even though it is one package one fee for some things, if you have two loans that you want to break, you may be stung by two deferred establishment fees and two discharge fees.

As a rule, the more you are borrowing and the more complex your borrowing, banking, financial planning and insurance needs are, the greater your benefit will be from taking a pro-pack.

Sweep to save aka "the sweeper"

This is an interest saving strategy which can be quite powerful for some people, moderately beneficial for others and disastrous for many. For every dollar it might save you, it could cost you three more when you get it wrong. And I have seen a LOT of people get it wrong which might be why it is so popular with the merchants.

Pitching Sweep to save allows a clever salesperson to appear skilful, knowledgeable, helpful and on the borrower's side by letting them in on a hot interest saving tip. Yet this double edged sword often sees unwitting borrowers stuck in debt for longer and paying a viciously higher rate of interest for the privilege.

For this reason alone, I deliberated over whether the sweeper should appear in Mortgage Free, Debt Free at all.

I finally decided to offer it up to you so you can get the Sweep to save right if you are one of the few that can benefit from it. However I also wanted to warn you about it if you are more likely the type that will lose rather than save money when attempting this strategy.

As long as your loan allows unlimited extra repayments and has fee-free redraw you can turn the sweeper on whenever you want. Some may argue that having a transactional offset account makes Sweep to save a little easier to manage, but that ain't necessarily so. Anyhow, let's get on with it.

Sweeping is the act of clearing the full balance of a credit card every month. That's full balance as in the amount of money you spent the month before, not paying the minimum amount payable or the minimum amount plus a bit. It's paying the full balance, never a cent less.

This means you must be a very disciplined person to make the Sweep to save work at all.

Ummm no. A vacuum cleaner won't work better. It's a different kind of sweeping.

To find out how high the risk is that like many you will get it wrong, ask yourself 5 simple questions. Answer them based on your money management behaviour over the past four or more years. BE HONEST.

1. Do you ever find yourself with little or no money the day before your next payday?

2. Have you ever taken an interest free deal only to end up paying interest because you couldn't pay the credit out within the interest free period?

3. Do you ever roll balances forward on your credit card by paying just the minimum payment or the minimum plus any extra you can afford?

4. Do you find it difficult to save?

5. Have you ever been tempted to take advantage of balance transfer promotions from credit card companies?

If you have answered yes to even one of these questions, you should steer clear of this strategy and move on to the next section before you start bleeding money. The more times you answer 'yes', the more likely it is that the Sweeper will not work for you and you should seriously think twice before attempting it.

Still reading huh? Okay then. The Sweep to save works by maximising offsets from any cash you have earmarked for bills and general spending. You must strictly follow eight golden rules:

1. Deposit all income either directly into your mortgage or into a 100% offset account.

2. Use a small credit card that offers at least 40 days interest free to pay any bills or expenses.

3. Pay the full balance of your credit card on the last day possible each and every month.

4. Never withdraw cash from your credit card.

5. Avoid using cash for purchases.

6. Reduce non credit card electronic transfers as much as possible.

7. Watch out for and avoid credit card surcharges (Caltex service stations are good at charging these).

8. Keep the limit on your credit card as low as possible at all times.

By following the eight golden rules, many of your bills, such as fuel for your car, are paid using your credit card which accesses money from your credit card company. However you only pay your credit card once a month and this could be up to a month after you paid your bill with someone else's money.

In the meantime the money that once would have disappeared from your account the instant that you fuelled up now offsets the interest charged on your mortgage. It continues to reduce your interest right up to the moment you spend it to repay the credit card company that picked up your fuel tab a month or so earlier.

Provided you stick to the eight golden rules, you won't be charged interest by the credit card company either. You get an interest saving for the now extended time that your petrol money offsets your mortgage, yet incur no charge for using the credit card company's money in the meantime. For most transactions, this is a microscopic amount of free money, however as the same idea is true for many other bills such as groceries, phone bills and council rates this microscopic free money can add up over time. The more of your general spending you can put on the card, the larger your potential interest savings will be and yes, if you stick with the eight golden rules, Sweep to save will work. If you stick to those rules.

However you should put aside the excitement of this new found free money and take a look at the share prices of credit card companies or the companies that own them. None of them are struggling which is a very clear message that even though all of them offer credit cards with interest free days, most people don't wind up spending interest free money. Otherwise the credit card companies would simply go broke.

To make the Sweep to save work at all, you must pay the full balance of your credit card off each month, every month. Miss just one month and you will set yourself back around four months worth of savings.

Miss repeatedly and although you might think you are staying on top of things because you are making minimum repayments or perhaps a little more, you will actually be costing yourself between two and four times the interest you should be paying. Yikes.

If you find yourself in this position, it can quickly make an interest mountain out of what seems like a molehill and you should consider cancelling your credit cards and abandoning this strategy as soon as possible.

The other trap you must continue to keep a sharp eye out for is the credit card surcharge (sometimes called a transaction charge).

Some time back, it became legal for suppliers who 'welcome' credit cards to charge you an extra fee when you pay with your credit card. Although these charges may appear to be quite small (for example, 1%, $2, 2% etc) they often grossly exceed the savings you will make from the interest offset on your mortgage. In the simplest of terms, paying credit card surcharges often cost more that you could ever hope to save.

If you're like me and you don't like going backwards simply to profit others, you should either avoid using a credit card where surcharges apply; or take the time to work out the point where a surcharge is still worth paying. The latter is really only for those people who are mathematically agile and seriously stingy. Yep, that's me again (the seriously stingy part). If you're not that concerned with getting debt free faster, then skip ahead to the end of this section on page 221. For the quick and the curious, you can understand the point where a surcharge takes you backwards in a few simple steps.

First, divide your mortgage interest rate by 12. If the surcharge is greater than the result, then it is more economical to park the card for that purchase and pay with cash or EFTPOS from another account.

For example, if the interest rate on your mortgage is 9% then:

Max = Your Mortgage Interest Rate / 12

9% / 12 = 0.75%

Your Maximum Acceptable Surcharge is 0.75%

In this example, if the surcharge is 1%, you should not use your credit card. If it was 0.5% then it is not so bad, but it still bites into your interest saving.

You might also find suppliers like Bigpond that charge a flat rate surcharge (sometimes called a processing or credit card fee). To work out whether you should use your card in this situation, simply multiply the amount of the bill by your Maximum Acceptable Surcharge.

For example, your insurer may charge $2 to debit your insurance premiums at $60 per month which means:

Max = Maximum Acceptable Surcharge x Bill Amount

0.75% x $60 = 45 cents

Your Maximum Acceptable Fee = 45 cents

In this example, the $2 you will be charged exceeds your Maximum Interest Saving of 45 cents, so it is not worthwhile taking this option.

If this sounds like too much stuffing about, then just avoid using a card to pay any biller or supplier that charges a credit card surcharge, processing or credit card fee. The risk outweighs the reward.

Oh, and always watch out for tiny little signs around cash registers and on fuel bowsers that alert you to these charges. Either pay cash, use EFTPOS or go to another shop.

If you do decide to give the sweeper a go, make sure you stay honest and monitor your progress. Make sure you <u>always</u> follow the eight golden rules.

If you miss just one sweep, get out before it's too late.

You'd be amazed how many miserable mortgaged people I've met that have been brought to their knees by a credit card. Please don't be one of them.

Cashback Deals

If you are even slightly serious about making more of your money, it's a no-brainer to get a cashback deal on your loan if you can. Getting lender commissions paid to you by your broker on a regular basis in combination with The Free Money Strategy is the only risk-free, no extra effort way to save money on your mortgage.

Even if you don't follow any other interest saving strategy, you can still come out in front by around $57,000 on the average mortgage. Bolt on the rest of the tips in Mortgage Free, Debt Free, and you will get debt free sooner. A lot sooner.

However, like all things mortgage, there are some pitfalls to watch out for when choosing a mortgage broker that promises to share their commission. After all, you are still dealing with a debt merchant.

Granted brokers offering cashback may be more committed to your interests or at least more willing to put their money where their mouths are than others, but you should still take care. Like those that don't share commissions, some cashback brokers have a lower risk of being affected by commission bias, but others have a higher risk and it's hard to tell the difference.

No matter what, none of them are in it for love.

To get the greatest benefit from The Free Money Strategy, payments must be:

1. Reliable.

2. Paid to your mortgage monthly.

3. 100% of the trail commission paid by the lender.

With the amount of money that these payments and The Free Money Strategy can save you, it's worth taking a little extra time at the beginning to make sure you get it right. As Mum says, "if it's worth doing, it's worth doing right".

Reliability

Payment of trail commission by a lender to a broker is well protected by contract law with contracts worth millions and tens of millions of dollars. The value of these contracts means there is a healthy respect between parties and disputes are easily resolved.

If your broker promises, but then doesn't share their commission, you're out before the game begins. You can complain about it and maybe even sue, but that's about it. Selection of a reliable cashback broker from the outset is important, if not critical. A borrower's agent is able to help you with this as they don't take kickbacks from anyone, including brokers. However if you want to go it alone, there are some not-so-common sense tips that can help you achieve the best results.

While you can never be completely certain of your broker's reliability for making payments to you in the future, there are a few simple questions you can ask that should help you get a better feel:

1. How long have you been paying commission cashbacks to borrowers?

   If they just started last month then they have less proven history than a business that has done it for five or more years.

2. Is this a company-wide practice or is it a once-off special deal?

   You should be wary of once-off deals because it is very easy for the broker to back down on their word once they make the sale.

3. Is the Cashback Agreement between Head Office and me?

   If the answer to this question is no, then you may have a situation where Head Office can stop or never even start your payments, no matter what your individual broker promises.

4. Has the business ever failed to make a commission payment?

Make sure you get the answers to these questions in writing or by email before you commit to anything.

Cashback Payments: More Frequent = Larger Savings

It should be quite obvious that the key to maximising interest savings is getting these payments into your loan account as quickly and as often as possible. As lenders pay trail commissions monthly you should be able to have them paid to you on a monthly basis as well, although this is not possible with all cashback mortgage brokers.

Lowering the cashback payment frequency to quarterly will reduce the effectiveness of The Free Money Strategy and dropping back to once or twice a year reduces your savings even further.

Receiving cashback payments monthly also means you have much less at stake if a reliability problem surfaces. If your broker pays you monthly and they miss a payment, you only have one month's payment at risk. If the broker pays you annually and you miss out on a single payment, you could lose twelve months commission instead of just one. This could easily be well on the way to $1,000.

Monthly cashback payments are ideal; quarterly payments are less ideal and half yearly or annual payments are even less ideal again. However all of them blitz no cashback payments when it comes to getting mortgage free faster.

You can learn more about cashback mortgage brokers by visiting www.cashbackdeals.com.au.

The Claytons 100%

Beware the Claytons 100%, you know, the 100% you get when you're not really getting 100%. Although there are a couple of different ways your commission payments can be skimmed, the three most common methods are underquoting lender commissions, taking a chunk out before they calculate your cashback or attaching a massive fee. All of these are easily avoided by a getting a credit quote.

For those too young to remember, Claytons was a non-alcoholic substitute for spirits such as bourbon, rum or scotch.

Claytons is to scotch as carob is to chocolate.

Its slogan was "the drink you have when you're not having a drink," which quickly became common slang as a term for something that's a poor substitute for the real thing.

If for some reason you decide not to get a quote, there are still a couple of straight forward steps you can take yourself.

Firstly, go to the KeyFacts website and look up lender commissions. You'll find a full list of typical rates which is updated regularly. If your mortgage broker is quoting a lower rate, they could be skimming.

Next, carefully look for brokerage fees in the appointment or Cashback Agreement. Ethical mortgage brokers will offer you copies of all agreements before they take an application from you so that everybody knows where they stand.

Commission payments from lenders to mortgage brokers include GST.

As this is a tax to be paid to the ATO, your broker is unlikely to include the GST component they receive.

Part IV: The beginning of the End

"You have to learn the rules of the game. And then you have to play better than anyone else."
Albert Einstein

Well, here you are. Congratulations. I hope you found the journey here quicker and more entertaining than you might have at first imagined. Although it's the end of Mortgage Free, Debt Free, it's really just the beginning of your journey to achieving 'The Great Australian Dream" and getting there debt free as quickly as possible.

I hope you have enjoyed your expedition here and that the knowledge and tools you have gathered along the way prove as invaluable to you as they have for thousands of other borrowers. Of course before I go, I need to blab on just a moment longer to tell you a few more, very important things…

Currency is King

Okay, this is not a Gordon Gecko, "Greed is good" rule. I don't mean currency as in dollars and cents; I mean currency as in now. Today.

When I sat down to write this book, interest rates were different to what they are now that you are sitting down to read it. Although the tricks, traps and techniques that merchants use will always be around, products and lenders will come and go. Relying on out of date information is perched somewhere between foolish and downright dangerous, so there is simply no reason to review products or recommend ideal loans, lenders or brokers in this book.

Similarly, there is no point for you to pick up last months magazine or newspapers to get the latest mortgage news or products. By the time an interest rate or a product review is printed, there is a good chance that it is already out of date. There's no clearer case of this than the one we learned about at the end of "There's no such thing as perfect" and remember, the costs can be horrendous.

Only use reliable, current information whenever you are making decisions that affect your mortgage. That means information you have collected directly from merchants yourself in a credit quote, or you have paid a borrowers agent to collect for you. If you found it free on the internet, or it was offered up as advice by a debt merchant, then, well…..

Of course current unimportant information that you don't understand is useless so you should always get objective credit quotes that meet the KeyFacts Standard. Remember, they're free for everybody to use and not getting them could cost you a bomb.

By the time you are reading this, new tricks and solutions have probably emerged. You can always send me an email at michael.lee@keyfacts.com.au for the latest pointers and news.

Don't ask, don't get

I know that reads like an overly simplistic statement, however it is a simple rule that has served me well through the years and I hope it works for you too.

Never be afraid, or feel stupid or pre-empt failure.

You have a right to the support, honesty and value that you have just finished reading about and that I argue for on behalf of borrowers throughout Australia. Although delivering this ideal is beyond the standard that the mortgage industry is generally willing to offer you today, you will always get what you settle for. For things to change, you must force the hand of the lenders, the brokers and their mates. You must ask.

The worst thing that can come from asking is that you don't get what you asked for. But then again you might.

So remember "Don't ask, don't get".

Get it in writing

Or as my dad always said, believe nothing you hear and less than half of what you see.

Many merchants will say whatever comes to mind if it gets them a step closer to a fat commission cheque, a bonus or simply keeps the branch manager off their backs.

While some might know what they are talking about and may actually be *trying* to look after you, the reality is you can never be sure. Proving a conversation is at best difficult and at worst, impossible so always get as much as possible in writing.

Often, just asking a merchant to put it in writing will cause a back pedal where they know the information is patently untrue and this in itself could be enough to save your bacon.

Remember:

- ✓ To make sure all of your questions are answered.
- ✓ Email can be a useful tool as it shows the sender's details and includes headers which can help prove the authenticity of the communication.
- ✓ Look out for wriggle room words such as might; may; generally; probably; should; and can. It is not always possible to give an absolute answer, however make sure the wriggle room being created is not something that can cost you money.
- ✓ Make sure the question you asked is the one that is answered and that you understand the answer.
- ✓ Get credit quotes before you make any application. Yes I know, I do go on.

Getting answers properly documented in writing can be tricky and take some time, which is why it may be more effective for you to have a borrowers agent handle that aspect. As a general rule, ignore all mass produced information from merchants such as flyers, websites and advertising as it:

- ✗ Is cleverly designed to convince you that they have the right mortgage for you.
- ✗ Won't exactly apply to you so the differences could be worth thousands of dollars or even tens of thousands of dollars.
- ✗ Will have been approved by a legal team and include sufficient disclaimers, disclosures and ambiguities to give your debt merchant plenty of wriggle room.

Of course getting it in writing doesn't mean it's true either, however it does give you something to use in a formal complaint or legal action if you wind up with something stinky.

No one is an island – Getting Help

You can tell when you have really understood Mortgage Free, Debt Free, because you feel like you've learnt a lot and feel cautiously confident.

When I sat down to write, I came to the desk with years of experience, a deep set knowledge and most importantly, a support team. I didn't have to do this alone and neither do you.

Although Mortgage Free, Debt Free should cover most things you encounter, it may not cover everything.

If you ever find yourself with a question or want current, reliable information please visit the KeyFacts website at www.keyfacts.com.au.

You are also welcome to email me anytime at michael.lee@keyfacts.com.au if you have any questions, ideas or feedback. It might take some time, but I always respond to emails from my readers and welcome you to make contact (yes, I know I only mentioned that a moment ago).

> *"The difference between what we do and what we are capable of doing would suffice to solve most of the world's problems."*
> *Mohandas Gandhi (1869 – 1948)*

Well, that's it. I'll shut up now. Thank you for having me. You now have enough knowledge to do it. It's up to you to apply it.

Be smart. Protect your interest!

Oh, there is one more part and it's called Damage Control which I hope you never need. I have included it though, just in case…

Part V: Damage Control

"Once you get on that downward spin, it's tough to break the cycle. There has to be a lot of damage control at this point."
Anonymous

I hope that you are reading this because you are enjoying the book enough to want to read it cover to cover. Most of what I have written so far is about side stepping tricks, traps and problems that will damage your financial health. Each of these is directly associated with decisions you make in choosing and managing your mortgage.

However there are a bunch of sideline issues that can creep up and clobber you if you don't watch out.

Damage control helps you spot and deal with these problems.

Cushioning credit stress

For the record, mortgage stress is a member of the credit stress family. Suffering from any kind of credit stress stinks and mortgage stress is no exception. It can do anything from cramp your lifestyle a little to destroying your wealth and home life along the way.

Hopefully, you have greatly reduced your chances of experiencing mortgage stress by following the simple steps in this book. Unfortunately, 'greatly reduced' is not the same as 'eliminated' especially if somewhere along the way you set aside the decades of lessons captured in Mortgage Free, Debt Free and wandered onto the 'Screw it let's do it' path. No matter how you arrived at this page, we should take a look at the best way to deal with mortgage stress just in case you find yourself experiencing it. Perhaps the first thing we need to understand is how will you know if you've got it?

It's pretty fair to say you are suffering mortgage stress if you have a mortgage and you:

- □ Mostly don't feel like you are getting anywhere;
- □ Are anxious about spending money or have cut back spending on things that you enjoy;
- □ Feel concerned at the prospect of interest rate increases;

Tick one of those boxes and you can safely say that you are at risk of, if not already suffering some degree of mortgage stress. Tick more than one and there's no maybe about it. You've got credit stress.

Before we go any further, if you have missed a payment, have fallen behind in payments or feel you are about to do one or the other of these, forget about reading this chapter. Contact the credit crisis hotline in your state or territory immediately, and then call your lender to discuss your options. There is a big difference between mortgage stress and a full blown mortgage crisis and the prospect of missing payments means you are entering or already in mortgage crisis. You need focused, professional help to resolve this situation and the sooner you act, the better your outcome will be.

Still reading? Good. I take it that means you are not in crisis so let's get back to mortgage stress. A popular industry definition says you are suffering mortgage stress if you are paying 35 percent or more of your income in mortgage repayments. Although that's a nice neat formula, it doesn't really work.

For starters, 35 percent is a kind of arbitrary number that some people handle fine whilst others crack at 30%. For some, just the thought of having such a large debt causes stress. After all, stress is an emotional, and therefore an individual response.

Mortgage stress may be triggered by a range of circumstances; however it becomes most topical when lenders increase their home loan rates. When you think about that, it doesn't really add up. If you have the average $379,000, 30 year mortgage, a 1% p.a. rate hike from 7% to 8%, which most people would consider extreme, increases your repayment by $260 a month - less than $9 a day.

While everything is honky dory, the sun is out, the sky is blue and you are easily covering your repayments, it's hard to imagine that you would experience stress over $260 a month. After all, that's basically a daily coffee and a chicken caesar wrap from the local take away. Yet for some people even this small increase can trigger mortgage stress. If you are one of these people, you probably feel like you are balancing on a financial knife edge.

To suffer mortgage stress you either:

1. Unexpectedly lost an income;

2. Unexpectedly gained an ongoing expense;

3. Failed to implement the tips and pointers in "Part II: How to Beat the Banks and the Brokers";

4. Made other bad decisions since taking your mortgage.

Worst case, you've done all four.

For many of the mortgage stress sufferers I have met over the decades, the main pressure comes from decisions made after they took a mortgage. More often than not, the straw that breaks the camel's back is unsecured personal debt. You know, the credit card that lets you overspend today and delay your regret for months or years down the track. Or it could be the interest free deal that still seems to punch a bigger hole in your budget since the interest rate on your mortgage went up. Although the mortgage is part of the pressure it is often not the real problem.

This really should be thought of as 'credit stress', although it often gets unfairly pinned on the poor old mortgage which is usually the largest single monthly payment. This makes it an easy target, but it's the wrong one.

Sadly, it's not uncommon for some people to spend 50% or more of their mortgage repayment covering unsecured debt. If this sounds like you, you're probably suffering 'credit stress' rather than mortgage stress, not that one feels any better than the other.

Regardless of your situation, subduing mortgage stress can only be achieved by;

1. Increasing your income; or
2. Reducing your expenditure; or
3. Increasing your income and reducing your expenses.

Increasing your income

If you plan to keep your property, increasing your income is by far and away the best way to beat credit stress, especially if you devote every cent of that extra income to paying off debt rather than expanding your lifestyle.

What you can do and how effectively you can do it will be incredibly individual, but here are some of the steps that have worked for other people.

- ☐ Sell stuff you don't use – Auction sites such as ebay offer a low cost and simple way to convert stuff in your closet to cash on your mortgage.

- ☐ Ask for overtime / look for part-time work – Credit stress is often brought on by rising interest rates which usually coincide with a busy economy and this in turn can create more work opportunities.

- ☐ Ask for a pay rise – If it's some time since your pay has been reviewed and you think you should be earning more money, ask. Be smart and check around the market to find out how much demand there is for your career type and how much extra money it could pay.

- ☐ Consider sharing – Is your property big enough to share with a border. This can be an easy way to pick up an extra couple of hundred dollars a week with very little effort.

- ☐ Seek shelter – Completely rent out your property. Is it possible to move in with friends or family whilst you ride out the storm? If so, talk with your accountant about tax deductions that may be available to you and how you can access them today instead of waiting until the end of the financial year.

Standard insurance policies usually don't cover damage caused by tenants.

If you rent your property out make sure to consider taking out Landlord Protection Insurance.

These policies will often replace your standard contents policy and extend coverage to damage caused by tenants, loss of rent and other important risks you need to protect against.

Reducing your expenditure

Sorry, but there is nothing even slightly interesting to write about here. There are plenty of books, web sites and magazines that will give you great tips on cutting back. They range from taking a packed lunch to work through to buying your meat wholesale.

For the most part you need to make a bunch of small changes to add up to big savings.

Big ticket items that could help save your bacon include:

1. Downgrade your car to something cheaper to run and lower in value. Taking the time to sell privately is usually worth an extra couple of thousand dollars in your pocket over trading it in or selling it through a dealer.

2. Consider "Debt Consolidation" carefully and make sure you think things through before you act.

3. Read "Mogadon for mortgage stress".

Although it may be a less than comfortable idea, you should give serious thought to the reasons for your current state of credit stress and ask yourself honestly whether you are able to fix them or you are simply delaying the inevitable.

If possible, engage a financial counsellor to help you maintain a good level of objectivity as you establish a realistic plan to deal with the future and also to keep regular track of your progress.

As you work at fixing your situation, remember that it is possible to make credit stress go away today only for it to return even worse tomorrow.

So be careful to fix problems, not just cover them over.

Debt consolidation

If the only debts you have are mortgages on property, you can safely skip Debt consolidation. However if you also have credit cards, store cards, interest free deals, personal lines of credit, car loans or personal loans, you need to read on.

Debt consolidation is often life changing and is simple to do which is why so many people consolidate debt every day. Of course we also know that all that glitters is not necessarily gold, so let's take a look at what consolidation is, why you should or shouldn't do it and how to get it right if you decide to go ahead.

Quite simply debt consolidation is the combining of several debts into a smaller number of facilities, preferably one. For people with property, this often means paying out higher interest personal credit with money borrowed under a lower interest mortgage loan. By consolidating your debts this way, merchants gleefully tell you that you can:

- Make your life easier by eliminating several different payments at different times and replacing them with one easy payment;
- Lower your monthly payments;
- Save thousands in interest by switching from a ridiculously high interest rate to a much lower mortgage interest rate.

Now I know I'm a tad cynical, but the 'single payment' benefit is a bit of a red herring. It's like the furniture salesman throwing in free fabric protection on your new lounge. You might take it as a part of the deal, but you wouldn't walk into a shop to buy fabric protection and get the lounge thrown in. It's a warm and fuzzy feel good bonus designed to titillate your interest and get you 'over the line'. With Bpay, internet banking; telephone banking and direct salary debiting; most people don't really get any advantage from the old 'single payment' sales pitch.

However the other two benefits are a completely different story. They are real and from a financial health perspective, they can be life changing. The catch is that you can't significantly lower your monthly payments AND still save thousands in interest. Although consolidation could be an important step in reclaiming control of your money there are three vital facts you must understand before you leap into the dark abyss:

1. Debt consolidation is the quick fix, yo-yo diet of finance – many people who do it, often wind up in worse shape a year or two down the track.

2. If you need to consolidate debt you are already being beaten at the credit game. Your opponents are the banks and their expert friends who 'helped' you into debt so they can silently nip money from your pocket. However you are not losing a credit 'game' so much as you are losing money and the time it takes you to earn that money.

3. Choosing debt consolidation to lower your payments means you are still being beaten by the banks and the brokers, just different banks and different brokers.

Debt consolidation to save interest

Let's take a quick look at a basic example of Don who has accrued credit card debt of $25,000. (Only a few years ago that amount would have shocked me, nowadays I'm shocked when it's less. Big credit cards, car loans and not so interest free deals seem to be everywhere.)

Credit card companies generally insist on a minimum payment of two to three percent of the card balance each month and in Don's case, his minimum is $500 a month. The interest rate on his card is 16.50% and the rate on his mortgage is 7.15%.

Faced with these numbers, most people calculate a potential interest saving of almost 9.5% and on the surface this seems like a really big saving. However even with a rate difference like 9.5%, many people wind up paying a lot more interest after consolidating debt to their mortgage. This happens when people deliberately go for the "Lower payments" benefit or unthinkingly default to the minimum mortgage payment. These lower payments then spread the repayment term from a few years on a personal loan or credit card to 25 or 30 on their mortgage. Although you may get a lower rate of interest; you pay it for a much, much longer period and the longer you take, the more interest you will pay. To understand how significant this extra cost is, let's get back to Don.

In Don's case, his minimum monthly repayment falls from $500 on his credit card to just $168 when consolidated to his mortgage, creating an extra $332 in 'headroom' each month. This sets up a three way trap.

The first is when merchants promote the $332 as a "saving" without warning you of the actual extra cost. You know the ads. You might have read them as testimonials on web sites, maybe even heard them on radio or watched them on TV. "I went to XYZ and they got me a lower rate and saved me $1,000 a month!" When you encounter this claim without a warning on how much extra interest you will pay, it is an alarm bell ringing that the first trap has been carefully set.

The second is that the lower payment gives Don a feeling of being back in control and having extra spending capacity, which many borrowers then consume. It is this feeling that triggers the "yo-yo diet of finance" effect. Before Don knows it; his credit card has started to climb again, he's taken out the odd interest free deal and he accepts the limit increases offered to him by the bank.

The third trap is that even if Don doesn't yo-yo, he still pays more than double the interest he would have paid if he didn't consolidate and simply continued paying off his card at the minimum required repayment.

However, the upside is you can save a lot of interest by consolidating if you don't reduce your regular payment.

If, after consolidating, Don continues to pay the $500 a month on his mortgage, he would save around $13,000 in interest compared with paying the required $500 a month on his credit card.

Remember, that's a $13,000 interest saving on a $25,000 debt. Don would also slash the time it takes him to completely repay the debt by 30%. Needless to say that both of these results are very worthwhile.

WARNING:

If you are having trouble making minimum repayments, you should avoid taking drastic steps such as debt consolidation without first speaking with a financial counsellor about your individual situation.

Although it can be more stressful, having several smaller debts means you can negotiate with creditors individually and are more likely to receive a compassionate outcome because smaller amounts are involved.

If you cannot afford to pay at least 10% above your minimum monthly payments, you might be heading for severe financial pressure and you should make contact with an independent financial counsellor sooner rather than later.

For details of financial counselling services in your area call the national telephone hotline on 1800 007 007 or visit the Federal Governments Commonwealth Financial Counselling (CFC) Directory at: http://www.fahcsia.gov.au/sa/families/progserv/Pages/cfcp-cfcp_directory.aspx

Debt consolidation to reduce payments

Okay, so in taking a look at Don's situation, we have already seen that by using debt consolidation; he can reduce his monthly payments by $332. If you are suffering credit stress, having any extra cash on hand could be the break you need to regain control of your money as well as your peace of mind.

However before you race off to tap into lower payments, it is crucial to understand that this headroom comes at a very large, very real cost. For Don, the $332 a month headroom costs him more than $31,000 in extra interest on a $25,000 debt. Ouch.

By focussing on the lower repayment; calling the repayment difference a 'saving' and leaving out warnings about the actual cost, merchants entice you to join the dots between "lower rate" and "lower payment". This may lead you to think you can take the lower repayment and will still save plenty on interest too, however you won't.

Lower payments always mean you pay far more interest and you will spend more time in debt than you probably need to. Both of these outcomes mean better profits for the merchants. In isolation neither outcome profits you.

However for some people, opting for lower repayments is a necessary evil and if this sounds like you, make sure you calculate the cost of this decision before you sign up.

Approach	*Interest cost*	*Time with debt*
1. Continue to repay credit card at $500 per month	$17,582	7 years 2 months
2. Consolidate to the mortgage, continuing $500 per month payment	$4,768	5 years
3. Consolidate to the mortgage then reduce payments to minimum required ($168)	$35,858	30 years 1 months

Three ways of repaying Don's $25,000 credit card debt. Based on credit card interest rate 16.50% and a mortgage interest rate of 7.15%

So, before we get into the right way to consolidate, let's just do one final check and take a moment to consider if debt consolidation is the right idea for you. Ask yourself these basic questions:

1. Is the main reason you are consolidating debt to lower your payments?

2. Are you suffering severe credit stress i.e. you have or are likely to miss repayments?

3. Does the loan you are consolidating to have the same or higher interest rate as the debts you are consolidating?

4. Are you consolidating to a mortgage where you already owe 80% or more of the value of your property?

Although there is no hard and fast rule, the more times you answered 'Yes', the greater the risk that debt consolidation will worsen your financial situation. This doesn't automatically mean you shouldn't consolidate, it just means you should approach the idea more cautiously. Assuming you are still interested in consolidating debt, let's take a look at the best ways to go about it.

The right way to consolidate debt – Step 1

There are two parts to successful debt consolidation, sorting out your debt and sorting out your mindset. Of these, sorting out your mindset is most important yet it is also the most often overlooked by many people in the hands of clever merchants.

Step 1 – Sort out your mindset

Debt consolidation should only ever be undertaken if you change your attitude towards credit. The need to consolidate debt is a warning bell that you are going backwards and the larger the number or size of the debts, the louder that bell should be ringing. If you don't modify this behaviour, you are a prime candidate to yo-yo so before we talk about repairing the damage you've already done, let's stop the damage you might do in the future. Step 1 is to sort out your mindset by:

1. Refusing any more credit until you completely pay off all non-property debt and your consolidation loan (we'll cover that in a moment).

2. Cutting up the cards today.

3. Make every decision count toward becoming mortgage free.

Step 2 – Set your structure, summarise your position

For debt consolidation to have maximum benefit you should combine all non-property debts into a single loan with a lower interest rate. Unless you completely ignored every aspect of Mortgage Free, Debt Free, rates don't get much lower than the one you are paying on your mortgage. This usually makes consolidating non-property debts to a mortgage the most cost effective option.

However the next big mistake borrowers make is to 'top up' their mortgage or if their limit allows, draw extra funds out of their existing loan to pay out the other debts. The smaller, high interest debts suddenly disappear and your mortgage bloats just a little or perhaps not at all, creating a new problem, out of sight, out of mind. This makes it much easier to inadvertently slip back into bad credit habits.

To prevent this from happening to you, the debts you wish to consolidate must remain visible, manageable and independent of your current mortgage. However that doesn't mean you want to fluff around with multiple payments or different internet banking logons and it definitely doesn't mean you want to pay any extra for the privilege. Fortunately, you can achieve all this by creating a 'split' which can then be used as your 'consolidation loan'. A split has its own statements, loan term and payments allowing you to monitor and manage it separately to your existing mortgage even though it has the same interest rate. Provided you took the advice in "Things you might not know you need" your mortgage will easily handle this.

Consolidating debt as a separate split is a healthy reminder of how vulnerable you are to letting credit get the better of you. It also helps you see how quickly you are, or are not fixing the problem. For investors, this approach has the added bonus of allowing rent payments to be deposited where they do you the most good and to set automatic transfers to cover repayments of any investment loans as they come due.

So let's talk about sizing up your consolidation loan.

It's about now that you might want to make yourself a strong cuppa or if you are so inclined, keep a good stiff drink on hand. The next thing you need to do is list everything you owe, noting your limits, balances, interest rates and minimum monthly payments.

You then add up all debt that has an interest rate higher than your mortgage and the total of these debts will be your 'consolidation loan'. Make sure you do this step yourself and with your partner if you have one. As clunky or confronting as this exercise may seem, it is an important part of the process as it shows you how much you need to borrow for the consolidation loan. More importantly it helps you appreciate the results of the mindset that got you here in the first place as well as giving you an idea of where you will wind up if you don't change your attitude towards credit.

Written on the page in front of you, should now be the amount you will owe on your consolidation loan and the amount you owe on your mortgage. Time for that good stiff drink. Add the balances of your consolidation loan and your mortgage together to learn just how much you actually owe. If the total amount you owe is:

- Less than 80% of the value of your property, you are in for a relatively smooth 'debt consolidation ride'.

- More than 80% of the value of your property you will pay Lenders Mortgage Insurance to consolidate your loan and that price could be hefty so you should proceed with caution.

- More than 90% you will pay a Lenders Mortgage Insurance premium that sits somewhere between ugly and horrific. You will also face real challenges and limitations getting a consolidation loan on your mortgage approved. You may only be able to consolidate some of your debt and are likely to be subject to exceptionally high LMI premiums which can destroy any potential interest saving. You should proceed with extreme caution and think seriously about not proceeding at all.

If you are still determined to consolidate, you should now add up your current monthly payments for all debts that you will roll into your consolidation loan. Write down the words 'current payment' and the total that you have just calculated immediately next to them. Do not include the repayment for your current mortgage in this total.

Remember, your current payment does not include your existing mortgage repayments. Yes, I know you just read that, but it's important.

Step 3 – Decide your objectives

Now that you can see the amount you owe and the amount you are paying out on this debt every month, it's time to decide your plan of attack. What is most important to you? Is it to:

1. Improve your lifestyle in the medium term by getting mortgage free, debt free as soon as possible; or

2. Improve your lifestyle in the short term by lowering your repayments.

Although you can choose both, each of these priorities works against the other. To get mortgage free, debt free as soon as possible you shouldn't reduce your current repayments at all. However to get the best improvement in your short term lifestyle, you want the biggest immediate reduction in repayments you can get. This means making minimum repayments only so you will stay in debt for the longest possible time, paying a massive interest bill for the privilege. As an idealist who has lived through these decisions, I choose Option 1 over Option 2 because the medium term always arrives a lot faster than you think. However your circumstance and mindset may drag you toward Option 2.

If you agree with me and have made up your mind to get debt free as soon as possible, then you can jump ahead to Step 4, you're already done here. If like the captain of the Titanic you have decided full steam ahead and damn the iceberg and you will only pay the minimum repayment, then you can jump ahead to Step 4 as well. However if you are still undecided, or are thinking of doing a little bit of both, there is one other thing you need to do. Set your own payment.

The simplest way to set your own payment is to use any old online mortgage calculator entering your loan amount, current interest rate and the number of years you want to owe money on your consolidation loan (the loan term). If you start off by setting your loan term at 30 years, you will be able to see the minimum repayment, maximum cost result.

You should then set the loan term at 5 years which for most people will be very close to the maximum repayment, minimum cost result.

Although most mortgage calculators will work out the repayment for you, only a handful will work out your interest cost. When making this important decision, you should know the cost of your options. If the calculator you are using doesn't show the total interest cost, don't worry, it's pretty simple to work out. Just use this formula for principal and interest repayments:

(Repayment x Number of Payments) – Loan Amount

Or use this one for interest only payments:

(Repayment x Number of Payments)

For example, say you entered a loan amount of $35,000, chose a loan term of 30 years with monthly repayments and the calculator said your principal and interest repayment was $225. The first thing to work out is the Number of Payments:

Number of payments = Loan Term x Payments per year

= 30 x 12

= 360

Then:

Total interest cost = (Repayment x Number of Payments) – Loan Amount

= ($225 x 360) - $35,000

= ($81,000) - $35,000

= $46,000

Try a few different loan terms until you find the right personal balance between the size of the loan payment and the extra interest cost you will pay for taking that lower repayment.

> If you take a 30 year loan term, but repay that loan based on a 15 year repayment, your total interest cost will be the same as if you take a 15 year loan term and repay the minimum required repayment.

Step 4 – Shop it

Get a quote from your existing lender for the fees to establish your "consolidation loan" split. You should also shop your soon to be larger mortgage with other merchants as the larger loan and competition changes since you took out your original loan may mean there are better deals to be had. Before you do, take a moment to revisit:

- "Avoid common, costly mistakes" – page 57.
- "Step 2: Choose your weapons" – page 97.
- "Step 3: Design your debt" – page 119.
- "Step 4: Turning the tables" – page 159.

If you do not want to hire a borrower's agent to assist you with this, make sure each merchant provides a credit quote that meets KeyFacts Standard.

Step 5 – Get rid of it and stay clean

Remember, many people who consolidate fall back into old habits. Each time you consolidate debt to your mortgage, you are surrendering equity in your property. It's like trading a part of your house for that new couch, the latest TV, pair of shoes or a night out on the town. So before you reach for your credit card, ask yourself, "is this really what I want to do?"

Debt consolidation is like a pain relief tablet. It will not get rid of the real problem, but it can ease the symptoms to let you get on living more comfortably while you treat the underlying illness. Debt.

The only cure is to pay it off.

Mogadon for mortgage stress

Mortgage stress keeps people awake at night and Mogadon is a hypnotic drug used in the treatment of insomnia. Now I'm not actually suggesting you should take drugs to deal with mortgage stress, rather there are some steps you can take that could have a similar stress lowering, sleep inducing effect.

It's at this point that I absolutely hope you are reading on as a preventative measure to avoid mortgage stress, rather than because you are suffering from it. If you have done your best with each option in "Cushioning credit stress" as well as those in "Debt Consolidation" and are still suffering mortgage stress then short of selling your property, you have almost run out of options. This is the last one I know of that actually works. Having said that, it only provides temporary relief for up to 5 years. It does not, in itself, cure mortgage stress.

The final steps to relieving mortgage stress involve reducing current repayment pressures and heading off the risk of repayment pressure building back up in the short to medium term. These actions will cost you a lot more money in the long run, but they could also help you maintain your cool while you work your way through a bumpy patch.

Reducing repayment pressures

Switching your mortgage from principal and interest to interest only will reduce your monthly repayment. As an example, a $350,000, 25 year, principal and interest loan with an interest rate of 7.15% per annum has a monthly payment of $2,507.32.

Switching this loan to Interest only reduces your monthly payment to around $2,085.42 which puts $421.90 back in to your living money each month.

Now there are some very important points to remember:

1. I wrote 'switching' <u>this</u> loan to Interest only, not refinance to Interest only.

2. Stick with your existing lender to keep costs and paperwork down. The switching fee should only be a few hundred dollars.

3. Don't borrow any extra money along the way.

4. Interest only reduces your monthly payments by a little, but increases the amount of interest you pay by a LOT.

5. Make sure you use any money that this frees up for essential uses, not luxury items.

6. To reduce the cost of this safety net, continue to pay as much as possible.

7. Wherever possible use the extra headroom to protect against future mortgage stress by saving, not spending it.

Above all else, remember this approach is a Damage Control strategy designed to help you deal with the situation that you have already spent more money than you could afford to spend.

Future proofing

By reducing repayment pressures you will buy, yes buy, some relief from mortgage stress.

However should rates continue to rise; the noose will again begin to tighten. As you have already switched to Interest only, you will have fired off one of the last silver bullets you have. Mortgage stress will again rear its ugly head and you will have fewer weapons to subdue it with than you have today. The next one involves selling your property. Now could be the time to spend some money on insurance to lock your rate in.

Although fixed rates are almost always higher than variable, the switch to Interest only should be enough to allow you to also buy the safety of a fixed rate loan for the same or less than your old variable rate repayment.

There are some very important points to remember:

1. Time is usually of the essence. Read "Fix your mindset or your mortgage" before you do anything else.

2. Ask yourself how much protection you need. A three year fixed rate will be cheaper than a five year fixed rate, but if you don't think you will be out of the woods within three, five years fixed could be a better option even at a higher price.

3. Check the rate of your current lender against the market. If it is within a reasonable tolerance, then you are probably better off switching to fixed where you are to save time.

4. Think about leaving a small portion variable if your lender's fixed rate does not allow extra payments and redraw. This allows you to bank spare money and lump sums like your tax return cheque against your mortgage; save interest and still have that money at the ready for emergencies. A 'small variable portion' could be between $5,000 and $10,000.

5. Don't take a 50:50 fixed variable split.

Although you should safely be able to relax a little, don't get complacent. The strategies explained in "Mogadon for mortgage stress" are designed to temporarily reduce your mortgage stress and allow you to hold on to your property.

You simply must increase your income reliably and significantly before the Mogadon wears off.

Get Debt Free with a Snowball

Debt consolidation is never free from either cost or risk. If the savings aren't there or lenders won't allow you to do it or you'd simply prefer to shoot your debts dead where they stand, you need a good debt elimination strategy.

Although there are a number of different ideas you can deploy to eliminate debt, there is only one that I have found effective for most people.

Called the Snowball, it is a radically different approach to the traditional pyramid strategy. Snowball offers frequent reward and progress markers which should keep you on track to becoming debt free faster – and yes, this can include killing off your mortgage as well.

It is called the Snowball as it relies on a small monthly stake which rapidly gains momentum as each debt is paid out.

The first step is to list your debts, including the amount you owe (the balances) as well as each minimum monthly payment. Now add all of your minimum monthly payments together to get your 'total minimum monthly payment', and then work out 10% of that amount. Just 10% is all the extra commitment you need to make real change. This amount is the start of your snowball and is usually surprisingly small. For example:

	Limit	Amount owing	Min. Monthly Payment
Credit Card 1	$ 20,000	$ 15,000	$ 300
Credit Card 2	$ 5,000	$ 4,000	$ 120
Personal Loan	$ 12,000	$ 12,000	$ 400
Mortgage	$ 250,000	$ 250,000	$ 2,000
Total Minimum Monthly Repayment			$ 2820
Snowball = 10% of Minimum so			$282

Now that you have your snowball, the next step is to work out where to aim it.

In the traditional pyramid strategy, you start by attacking the debt with the highest interest rate which theoretically keeps your interest bill as low as possible. While this is a nice idea, it usually doesn't kill your debts as quickly or as regularly as the Snowball and without that regular feedback, many borrowers lose focus, commitment and interest. That's interest as in fascination as well as interest paid to lenders.

Snowball is about maintaining momentum, building on momentum and eliminating the debt. So the real question is which one can you kill the fastest?

To work this out, you need to find the Instalments Index for each debt and you can do this using a very basic formula:

$$\text{Instalments Index} = \frac{\text{Amount Owing}}{(\text{Payment} + \text{Snowball})}$$

Work down your list until you have worked out the Instalments Index for each debt. Your list should now look something like this:

	Amount Owing	*Payment + Snowball*	*Instalments Index*
Credit Card 1	$15,000	$300 + $282	25.8
Credit Card 2	$4,000	$120 + $282	9.95
Personal Loan	$12,000	$400 + $282	17.59
Mortgage	$250,000	$2,000 + $282	109.56

The debt with the lowest Instalment Index is the one where you should aim your snowball. In the meantime, you continue making just the minimum payments for the rest of your debts.

In the example, the first debt to get the snowball is Credit Card 2, which has an instalment index of 9.95. This means that you should completely pay this card out in just under a year unless it has an insanely high interest rate, in which case it may take an extra month or two. You will then be down to just 3 debts.

Remember Rule 4 from "Stick to your strategy" – Never reduce your repayments.

By maintaining your payments at the existing level, you now have a much larger snowball. You have the original 10% that killed your first debt and you can now add the repayment that would have gone onto Credit Card 2 to boost its debt killing power. This means your snowball is now $402 (120 + 282) and ready to go.

Redo your list just to make sure rankings have not mysteriously changed, and then aim your 42% bigger snowball at the debt with the lowest Instalments Index.

In the example, the next in line for the snowball treatment is the Personal Loan. Your larger snowball of $402 plus the minimum payment for the Personal Loan will eliminate it in a matter of months. Once that happens, you will have quickly grown your snowball to $802 to kill off the next one.

There are only two debts left in less than two years from when you packed your first snowball.

Had you used the same size snowball and followed the traditional pyramid strategy, the best you could hope for at this point in time is to have killed off just one of your debts - you would still have three to go. Worse still, you might not have killed off any at all. Blergh.

However, with the snowball strategy hammering away you will kill off the second last debt in less than a year. Then the only thing left is that mortgage, which really takes the guesswork out of where you need to aim next.

Perhaps the most surprising thing to nearly everyone is you will have achieved the result simply by increasing your current minimum repayment by 10%, carefully aiming your snowball and still living on almost all of the disposable income you currently enjoy.

Cut up the cards.

If you do keep a credit card, make sure it has at least 40 interest free days and the limit is no more than the amount you can repay each month. For most people, this should be around three weeks nett pay.

However if you think you 'need' a credit card, you are already in trouble again.

Try switching to 'cash only' for a few months. Easy credit helps you live beyond your means. Living without it, will give you a good sense of what your 'means' really is.

This really is it

Not wanting to sound like John Farnham, but this really is the end of the book. Besides a mandatory blurb about me and the references and sources sighted in Mortgage Free, Debt Free, there is no more.

I hope that you meandered to this page in your first read, never needed to read Damage Control, but read it anyway, laughed a little and learnt a lot along the way.

Most of all I hope that, as I wrote way back in the beginning, you apply what you have learned here. In no time at all, you will be on the path to becoming mortgage free and debt free, which is a wonderful destination.

I look forward to seeing you there and hope that you will email me about your adventures along the way.

References and Sources

In addition to the personal and professional experience of the author, Mortgage Free, Debt Free was compiled using the following references and sources.

Commission Rates and Lender Panels sighted throughout Mortgage Free, Debt Free.
See:
http://matesratesmortgagebrokers.com.au/mortgage-lenders/mortgage-broker-commissions/:

John Symonds quotes.
See:
http://www.aph.gov.au/hansard/reps/commttee/R11143.pdf

Consumer Credit information sighted as a source for "Comparison Rates… Last Drinks Gentlemen".
See:
http://www.creditcode.gov.au

Consumer Credit (QUEENSLAND) Amendment Act 2002 sighted as source for "Up yours coppa".
See:
http://www.creditcode.gov.au

Mortgage and Finance Association of Australia sighted as a source for "Shhh… CLEVER Wordsmiths at work".
See:
http://mfaa.com.au/default.asp?menuid=480

Property Report - AFG Property October 2005 sighted as a source for "Shhh… CLEVER Wordsmiths at work".
See:
http://www.financial-partners.biz/australian/hardcopy/australian_newsletter_oct05.pdf

Australian Finance Group December 2010 Mortgage Index Report sighted as a source for "Shhh… CLEVER Wordsmiths at work".
See:

http://corporate.afgonline.com.au/idc/groups/public/documents/web_content/mortgageindex-dec10-national.pdf

Mortgage Choice Prospectus 2004 sighted as a source for "Paying retail".
See:
http://www.mortgagechoice.com.au/downloads/file/Shareholders/MortgageChoiceProspectusAndApplication.pdf

Getting more from a lender, courtesy The Sunday Telegraph, sighted as a source for "Blind leaps of faith".

Australian Mortgage Industry Volumes 1 - 11,
JP Morgan and Fujitsu Consulting sighted as source for "Things you might not know you need".
See:
http://www/fujitsu.com.au

The Mortgage Broker Service Gap, Fujitsu Consulting sighted as a source for "Use a mortgage broker".
See:
http://www.fujitsu.com/downloads/AU/fujitsu_broker_research.pdf

Mortgage Stress- Tony Kryger, Statistics and Mapping, Parliamentary Library sighted as a source for "Cushioning credit stress".
See:
http://www.aph.gov.au/library/pubs/rn/2003-04/04rn16.htm

All financial models and calculations appearing in Mortgage Free, Debt Free were independently developed and tested by KeyFacts Australia Pty Limited.

Materials, tools and tips mentioned as available in this book can be found free of charge at the KeyFacts website.
See:
http://www.keyfacts.com.au

Index

About the Author

Michael Lee is a mortgage researcher, educator and freelance journalist. In late 2000 he began developing Australia's most controversial pro-consumer mortgage broker models before becoming Founder and Consumer Advocate for bSmart and Mates Rates Mortgage Brokers. He has also been a senior manager for a Top 3 multinational computer services company, responsible for hundreds of staff across the Asia Pacific Region in addition to the management and delivery of a multi-million dollar budget. Lee attributes his financial literacy, investment ability and success to a lifetime passion for property, an open heart and a cautious mind.

Lee's mortgage tips, research and articles have appeared in national magazines and numerous newspapers nationwide. He speaks on mortgage insights, consumer rights, industry ethics and other subjects. He has appeared on national television and radio and has also appeared before Federal Government Inquiries as a lobbyist for consumer rights. Lee is a full member of the Australian Society of Authors.

People, ethics, the environment and property are his professed passion and he continues to work actively in all fields. To date Lee has placed over 60 acres of native and regenerated forest in perpetual trust for the benefit of future generations with, he says, more to come.

A minimum of 20% of all author royalties and publisher profits resulting from Mortgage Fee Debt Free are donated to charity as a part of Lee's Save Yourself, Save a Child and Save the Planet campaign. Visit "Your Gift" at www.mortgagefreedebtfree.com.au for further information.

Made in the USA
Monee, IL
12 November 2026

68342113R00153